FORTRESS • 69

THE BERLIN WALL

and the Intra-German Border 1961–89

GORDON L ROTTMAN

ILLUSTRATED BY CHRIS TAYLOR

Series editors Marcus Cowper and Nikolai Bogdanovic

First published in Great Britain in 2008 by Osprey Publishing,
Midland House, West Way, Botley, Oxford OX2 0PH, UK
44-02 23rd St, Suite 219, Long Island City, NY 11101, USA
Email: info@ospreypublishing.com

Osprey Publishing is part of the Osprey Group.

Transferred to digital print on demand 2012

First published 2008
3rd impression 2010

Printed and bound in Great Britain

A CIP catalogue record for this book is available from the British Library

ISBN: 978 1 84603 193 9

Editorial by Ilios Publishing, Oxford, UK (www.iliospublishing.com)
Page layout by Ken Vail Graphic Design, Cambridge, UK (kvgd.com)
Index by Sandra Shotter
Cartography by The Map Studio, Romsey, UK
Typeset in Sabon and Myriad Pro
Originated by united graphic Pte Ltd, Singapore

Acknowledgements
The author is indebted to Paxton Williams, Glenn Allardyce, William C. Schneck, Burkhard Schulze,
and Dirk Rudolf 'Festus' Festerling for their assistance on this project.

Linear measurements
Distances, ranges and dimensions are given in the metric system. To convert these figures to the
US system the following conversion formulae are provided:

centimetres (cm) to inches: multiply centimetres by 0.39

metres (m) to feet: multiply metres by 3.28

kilometres (km) to miles: multiply kilometres by 0.62

The Fortress Study Group (FSG)
The object of the FSG is to advance the education of the public in the study of all aspects of
fortifications and their armaments, especially works constructed to mount or resist artillery.
The FSG holds an annual conference in September over a long weekend with visits and evening
lectures, an annual tour abroad lasting about eight days, and an annual Members' Day.

The FSG journal FORT is published annually, and its newsletter Casemate is published three
times a year. Membership is international. For further details, please contact:

The Secretary, c/o 6 Lanark Place, London W9 1BS, UK

Website: www.fsgfort.com

Imperial War Museum Collections
Some of the photos in this book come from the Imperial War Museum's huge collections which
cover all aspects of conflict involving Britain and the Commonwealth since the start of the
twentieth century. These rich resources are available online to search, browse and buy at
www.iwmcollections.org.uk. In addition to Collections Online, you can visit the Visitor Rooms where
you can explore over 8 million photographs, thousands of hours of moving images, the largest
sound archive of its kind in the world, thousands of diaries and letters written by people in wartime,
and a huge reference library. To make an appointment, call (020) 7416 5320, or email:
mail@iwm.org.uk.

Imperial War Museum www.iwm.org.uk

The Woodland Trust
Osprey Publishing is supporting the Woodland Trust, the UK's leading woodland conservation
charity, by funding the dedication of trees.

www.ospreypublishing.com

CONTENTS

THE BERLIN WALL AND THE INTRA-GERMAN BORDER 1961–89

INTRODUCTION

In 1980 I found myself in a newly organized long-range reconnaissance patrol company. After two years of training we were assigned to V Corps in Germany, although we remained in the United States. Our mission in the event of a Soviet invasion of West Germany (more correctly, the Federal Republic of Germany, or BRD) was to insert our 21 five-man reconnaissance teams inside East Germany (the German Democratic Republic, or DDR), establish 'hides' overlooking autobahns, and report the movements of the Soviet second operational echelon, the follow-on forces behind the initial assault. This required us to learn a great deal about conditions inside East Germany. Our teams would mostly be inserted and extracted by helicopter. But what if teams were unable to make contact with their pick-up? They would have to return to friendly lines on foot, which meant crossing the Intra-German Border (IGB) dividing East and West Germany. The IGB was designed to keep people inside East Germany.

The opinion of V Corps' G2 staff was that, following a Soviet invasion, the IGB barriers would all have been pushed down by the masses of Soviet armour, and as a result the border would be unmanned. We began to investigate, and found this was far from likely. Soviet forces would penetrate into West Germany on the main highways; the border fence would remain in place, and the Frontier Troops (*Grenztruppen*) would continue to man it as a control line. This would prevent East German civilians from heading west, serve as a catch line for Warsaw Pact stragglers and deserters, and hamper the cross-country infiltration and exfiltration of NATO special operations forces and downed air crewmen. We thus began an intense study of the IGB, and in the process I was able to visit it and find out how to penetrate it.

Almost everyone is familiar with the 206km-long Berlin Wall, often simply called 'the Wall' (*die Mauer*), which completely surrounded West Berlin. The city lay deep behind the border between East and West Germany, making West Berlin an island of democracy deep inside a totalitarian state. In contrast, few are aware of the equally well-sealed, 1,401km-long

A German civilian looks at a vast painting of Stalin on the Unter-den-Linden in Berlin, 3 June 1945. (IWM BU 8572)

Intra-German Border between the DDR and BRD, which ran along the original 1945 demarcation line (*Demarkationslinie*) separating the three Western Allies' occupation zones from the eastern Soviet Zone. The BRD called this the Intra-German Frontier (*Innerdeutsche Grenze*) or simply the Land Frontier (*Landgrenze*). In the DDR it was the German-German Frontier (*Deutsch-Deutsche Grenze*). With the exception of the Korean Demilitarized Zone, the IGB was the most heavily secured border in the world.

THE ORIGINS OF DIVISION

In 1946, at Westminster College in Fulton, Missouri, Winston S. Churchill gave a speech that included a soon to be famous metaphor: 'An Iron Curtain has descended across the Continent. Behind that line lie all of the capitals of the ancient states of central and eastern Europe ... All these famous cities and the populations around lie in the Soviet sphere and all are subject ... to a very high and increasing measure of control from Moscow.'

The Iron Curtain Churchill was referring to stretched 6,800km from the north of Finland to the Black Sea. Its line was marked by the borders of the Soviet satellite states of Poland, Czechoslovakia, Hungary, Bulgaria, Romania, and the Soviet Occupation Zone (*Sowjetische Besatzungszone*) in eastern Germany. The USSR installed Communist governments in these states and militarized them. The goal was to establish a buffer zone to protect the USSR from perceived Western aggression. The USSR swore never to allow a repeat of the German 1941 invasion that devastated the country and cost over 20 million lives.

The North Atlantic Treaty Organization (NATO) was established by Western European and North American countries in April 1949. NATO unified the member nations for collective security from increasing Soviet intimidation, which manifested itself chiefly in the June 1948–May 1949 Berlin Blockade. This was a blatant attempt to drive American, British, and French occupation forces from the former capital inside the Soviet Occupation Zone, despite being in clear violation of the 1945 four-power Potsdam Agreement. In June 1948 the autobahn, railway and barge routes from West Germany were blocked by Soviet troops. However, they could not block the air routes without shooting down aircraft, and the Berlin Airlift (*Luftbruecke*) began. Food, coal and medical supplies were brought in solely by air, a process that continued through to September 1949 – even though the blockade had been lifted in May when the Soviets abandoned their 322-day restrictions.

The Deputy Supreme Commander in Chief of the Red Army, Marshal G. Zhukov, the Commander of the 21st Army Group, Field Marshal Sir Bernard Montgomery, Marshal Sokolovsky and General K. Rokossovsky of the Red Army leave the Brandenburg Gate after Montgomery has decorated the Russian generals in a ceremony on 12 July 1945. (IWM TR 2913)

British and American air force officers consult a chart depicting routes and altitudes of all aircraft in and out of West Berlin during the Airlift in 1948. (IWM TR 3841)

The origins of the division of Germany go back to the February 1945 Yalta Conference. A Committee on Dismemberment of Germany was to be established to decide whether Germany was to be divided into several nations, and if so, what borders and inter-relationships the new German states would have. With the disintegration of German central authority at the war's end, Allied commanders were responsible for civil administration in their areas. German armed forces had surrendered in early May 1945, but the German government was not dissolved until the following month. The Allied Control Council was established in August to oversee the country's administration. Numerous orders were given to carry out de-Nazification and demilitarization, as well as everyday civil administration directives. At the same time, the Potsdam Conference divided Germany into four occupation zones: British in the north-west, American in the south, French in the south-west, and Soviet in the east. The US Zone bordered part of the Soviet Zone and Soviet-controlled Czechoslovakia. The comparatively smaller French Zone lay adjacent to its own borders and did not abut the Soviet Zone. Large areas of eastern Germany, namely Pomerania, Silesia, Danzig and East Prussia, were ceded to Poland and Austria was separated from Germany.

What would become West Germany encompassed 251,124km^2 and East Germany 108,298km^2. East Germany's population was about a third of that of West Germany, with many being refugees from lands ceded to Poland. As a point of comparison, in the mid-1970s West Germany's population was about 61,200,000 while the East had 17,100,000. The populations of the two Germanys were actually increased immediately after the war owing to the expulsion of ethnic Germans from the USSR, Poland, Czechoslovakia, Hungary, Romania and Yugoslavia. While East Germany possessed considerable industry, the West boasted much more, especially since most of the eastern industrial machinery was removed to the USSR as war reparations.

East and West Germany, 1989

Legend:
- ★ National capital
- Sector/Zone boundary
- Intra-German Border
- ① British Sector
- ② French Sector
- ③ American Sector
- ④ Soviet Sector
- ① British Zone
- ② French Zone
- ③ American Zone
- ④ Soviet Zone

0 — 100 miles
0 — 100km

DENMARK

BALTIC SEA

SCHLESWIG-HOLSTEIN

MECKLENBURG-VORPOMMERN

③ BREMEN

HAMBURG
● Hamburg

③ ● Bremen

NEDERSACHSEN

POL

NETHERLANDS

① ● Hannover

BERLIN (WEST) ② ① ③ EAST BERLIN ④

④ BRANDENBURG

SACHSEN-ANHALT

EAST GERMANY

NORDRHEIN-WESTFALEN
● Essen

● Leipzig

● Dresden

SACHSEN

THÜRINGEN

Bonn ★

HESSEN

BELGIUM   WEST GERMANY

Frankfurt am Main ●

CZECHOSLOVA

RHEINLAND-PFALZ

LUXEMBOURG ②

SAARLAND

③

BAYERN

● Stuttgart

BADEN-WÜRTTEMBERG

②

● Munich

FRANCE

SWITZERLAND

AUSTRIA

Two days after construction on the Wall commenced, an NVA soldier, Hans Conrad Schuhmann, leapt over a barbed-wire fence into West Berlin, discarding his PPSh-41 submachine gun in the process.

Germany was roughly divided along old state (*Lander*) boundaries. The border course (*Grenzverlauf*), or 'trace' as it was called by US soldiers, separated the Western Allies' zones from the Soviet Zone, and was often locally adjusted by mutual agreement. The original states in the American and French zones were more numerous, but from 1949 to 1959 some were consolidated (see the map on page 7 and the panel on page 10)

The former capital of the Third Reich was likewise divided into four occupation sectors: the smaller French Sector in the north, the British one in west-central Berlin, the American one in the south, and the Soviet Sector encompassing approximately the eastern half. The Soviets were given a proportionally larger sector as they had paid for the capture of the entire city with over 360,000 casualties. It had been one of the most savage battles of the war, of barely two weeks' duration.

Berlin lay deep inside the Soviet Occupation Zone, separated from West Germany by 177km and only 89km west of the Polish border. The Baltic Sea (*Ostsee*) lay 180km to the north, with the Czechoslovak border a similar distance to the south. When West Germany was established, West Berlin became (an albeit detached) part of the Republic. Officially, the West Germans called it Berlin (West) to emphasize that the division was temporary. West Berliners had the full rights of other West German citizens, except they were exempt from military conscription, a hangover from the Four-Power agreements. In the mid-1970s West Berlin's population numbered 2,134,250 and East Berlin's 1,084,000. The population of greater East Berlin, which comprised inhabitants of the surrounding communities, increased the population on the East German side, including around West Berlin's 480km^2, which was unable to expand outwards.

In May 1949 the Federal Republic of Germany (FRG) – in German, *Bundesrepublik Deutschland* (BRD) – or West Germany, was established comprising the former British, American and French occupation zones (*Trizonia*), with its capital in Bonn. On October 7 the German Democratic Republic (GDR) – in German, *Deutsche Demokratische Republik* (DDR) – or East Germany, was established, but this was a mere Soviet puppet state (in 1974 its government declared it 'always and irrevocably connected with the Soviet Union'). It consisted of the Soviet Occupation Zone and its capital was East Berlin (*Hauptstadt der DDR*). The BRD was granted full sovereignty on 5 May 1955 and was accepted into NATO on 9 May.

Covertly snapped by a West Berliner, Volkspolizei (or Vopos) are shown erecting a barbed-wire fence on temporary concrete posts.

The BRD was authorized to raise armed forces, which would be under NATO command. The Federal Defence (*Bundeswehr*), consisting of the Army (*Heer*), Navy (*Marine*) and Air Force (*Luftwaffe*), was established on 12 November 1955. In response to this, the Warsaw Pact (see Elite 10: *Warsaw Pact Ground Forces*) – officially named the Treaty of Friendship, Co-operation and Mutual Assistance – was signed by the Soviet Bloc states on 14 May. On 1 March 1956 the National People's Army (*Nationale Volksarmee*, NVA) was raised, consisting of the Land Force (*Landstreitkräfte*), Air Forces/Air Defence

(*Luftstreitkräfte/Luftverteidigung*), People's Navy (*Volksmarine*), and Frontier Troops of the DDR (*Grenztruppen der NVA*).

In the Potsdam Agreement, the four occupying powers agreed to treat all of Germany as a single economic unit with some central administrative functions. The USSR soon disregarded this, establishing East Germany as a separate state. It would not be long before the Soviets pressed to include East Germany among the buffer states and to ensure Germany would never again become unified and pose a threat to the expansion of Communism.

The Wall rises

In May 1952 the border between the DDR and BRD and West Berlin was closed. Only the border between East and West Berlin remained open, allowing (at least until 1961) the city's inhabitants to cross from one zone to the other. Prior to the erection of the Berlin Wall, some 52,000 East Berliners worked in West Berlin (known as *grenzgänger*, frontier crossers). Forty per cent of their pay was in BRD Marks and the rest in Ostmarks. They had access to uncensored Western newspapers and watched movies banned in the East. The building of the Wall, which took place almost overnight in 1961, made international headlines and heightened tension between nations. The build up to the erection of the Wall began in October 1958 when Premier Khrushchev delivered the Berlin Ultimatum, demanding that the Western allies withdraw their forces from West Berlin within six months and that Berlin be declared a 'free city'. In February 1959 the USSR threatened to make a separate peace treaty with the DDR. This never occurred, and in June 1961 the Vienna meeting between President Kennedy and Khrushchev ended without any progress over the 'Berlin question', which led to the construction of the Wall.

ABOVE LEFT
The frontier crossed the Baltic coast just east of Priwall, West Germany. The Soviets emplaced chevaux-de-frise across the beach. These were later replaced by BRD red and white T-posts linked by chains. The absence of other barriers on the east side is due to the presence of kilometres of barbed-wire fences running parallel to the beach through the shoreline trees.

ABOVE RIGHT
Seen from the West German side, this road near Burggrub was cut by the Soviet occupation authorities by a barbed-wire fence, control strip, strapped-down pole gate, earth berm, ditch and more barbed wire.

BOTTOM LEFT
The zonal border ran the length of the River Ecker in the Harz and up to the reservoir, cutting the dam in half. The Soviets constructed a stout brick barricade studded by iron spikes across the middle of the concrete dam.

BOTTOM RIGHT
A soldier of the Soviet Border Troops urges a team of draft horses on as he harrows the control strip. The sagging, poorly strung barbed wire was common in many areas and did little to hinder escapees.

Germany divided

West German states (*Länder*) 1955–90

German	English
BRD	West Germany
Schleswig-Holstein	Schelswig-Holstein
Freie und Hansestadt Hamburg	Free and Hanseatic Hamburg
Niederschsen	Lower Saxony
Freie Hansestadt Bremen	Free Hanseatic City of Bremen[1]
Nordrhein-Westfalen	North Rhine-Westphalia
Hessen	Hesse
Rheinland-Pfalz	Rhineland Palatinate
Saarland[2]	Saarland
Baden-Württemburg[3]	Baden-Wurttemberg
Freistaat Bayer	Free State of Bavaria[1]
Berlin (West)	West Berlin

East German states (*Länder*) 1945–52[4]

German	English
DDR	East Germany
Mecklenberg-Vorpommern	Mecklenberg-Pomerania
Brandenburg	Brandenburg
Sachsen-Anhalt	Saxony-Anhalt
Thüringen	Thuringia
Saxhsen	Saxony
Berlin	East Berlin

Notes
[1] The titles 'Free Hanseatic' and 'Free State' are merely traditional.
[2] Integrated in the BRD in 1959 (Previously a French protectorate).
[3] Established 1951 by consolidating North and South Baden and North and South Wurttemberg.
[4] These states were dissolved by the DDR on 23 January 1952 and the country divided into 15 administrative districts (Bezirk) including East Berlin. The states were re-established upon reunification in 1990.

The two Germanys

West and East Germany and West and East Berlin were separated by the State Frontier between the DDR and the BRD and West Berlin (*Staatsgrenze der DDR zur BRD und West-Berlin*). Up to 200,000 citizens a year were leaving the DDR, with 160,000 fleeing between January and August 1961. Many were doctors, dentists, teachers, professors, engineers, lawyers, skilled industrial workers, and other professionals. The departure of young men and women, the most motivated and intelligent and the very future of the new socialist state, was of particular concern. This 'brain drain' was depleting the country of its best and brightest at a faster rate than it could train new professionals. Most were not fleeing food, housing and consumer goods shortages, rather political suppression, the forced collectivization of agriculture, the repression of private trade, and the loss of personal freedom. In 1948 the population of the Soviet Zone was 19 million; in 1960 it had fallen to 17 million. In contrast, the BRD's population had grown from 47 million to 55 million in the same timeframe.

While the DDR lost valuable human resources, their flight actually consolidated the Communist hold on the country: its strongest opponents had left. Those who remained lived a in a society discouraging initiative and independence, and lacking in genuine political responsibility. There was little prospect of internal change; uprisings had been brutally crushed in East Berlin (1953), Hungary (1956) and Czechoslovakia (1968) and the numerous internal security forces and counter-intelligence bodies exercised tight control.

Although the Berlin Wall came to symbolize the physical separation of the East and West, the real barrier between Western democracy and Communism was the IGB. The average East German had little idea of what the IGB was

BELOW LEFT
Czechoslovakia fortified its own borders. Here, Czechoslovak Border Troops repair a fence. A fence like this also faced the DDR's southern border. (US Army)

BELOW RIGHT
In the American Zone the US Army armoured cavalry regiments patrolled the border and maintained a few observation posts. Here cavalrymen scan the *Grenze*.

or what it looked like. It was a restricted zone and it was not discussed or pictured in the media. There were other walls dividing the East and West. Similar fortified borders and barrier systems snaked along the Czechoslovak border between the BRD and Austria. Hungary's more lightly fortified border faced Austria and Yugoslavia. Romania also bordered Yugoslavia, while Bulgaria faced Yugoslavia, Greece and Turkey. Even though the Warsaw Pact states were allies, their adjacent borders were also fenced and patrolled, as were their borders with the USSR.

With substantial NATO defence forces stationed in the BRD and West Berlin and Group Soviet Forces Germany situated in the DDR, Berlin and the IGB remained focal points of tension through the 50-year Cold War. The DDR declared itself as 'the only legal German state, to which the future of Germany belongs' and called itself 'the fatherland of the German people'.

ABOVE LEFT
The Stuttgart to Berlin rail line was cut in 1952. The bridge just off camera to the right was torn down, the track removed, and barricades built. The railway signal on the West German side is in the 'stop' position.

ABOVE RIGHT
This multi-line railway near Heinersorf was cut by simply pulling up the rails and sleepers. Barricades were erected on the West German side to the left (not shown).

CHRONOLOGY

1945

8 May Victory in Europe Day.

1946

30 June	The Soviet military administration declares the demarcation line between East and West Germany is safeguarded.
29 October	A 30-day Interzonal Pass (*Interzonenpass*) is required to travel between the different occupation sectors.
1 December	The 3,000-strong *Grenzpolizei* are established by the DDR to secure the west/east German frontier.
4 December	The occupation zone demarcation lines are established.

1948

	The *Grenzpolizei* increases to 10,000 men.
23 June	Berlin is divided into two currency zones.
24 June	The USSR begins the Berlin Blockade.
25 June	The Berlin Airlift begins.

1949

	The *Grenzpolizei* increases to 18,000 men.
12 May	End of the Berlin Blockade.

In the early 1960s double barbed-wire fences on concrete posts appeared. Anchor wires fastened to short wooden stakes secured both sides of the fences and angled wooden support posts reinforced the corner posts. The actual border was just a couple of metres outside the fence.

24 May	The Federal Republic of Germany (BRD – 'West Germany') is founded.
3 August	The first *Grenzpolizist* is killed on duty.
30 September	End of the Berlin Airlift.
7 October	The German Democratic Republic (DDR – 'East Germany') is founded.

1950

| June | The *Grenzpolizei* are given responsibility for the coast. |
| October | The *Grenzpolizei* are given responsibility for East Berlin and the DDR's borders. |

1952

| March–September | The 'Battle of the Notes'. Stalin proposes a reunified Germany if all powers withdraw and guarantee that Germany will be neutral and unarmed. |
| 26 May | The border between the DDR and BRD, and between the DDR and West Berlin, is closed. Only the border between East and West Berlin remains open. |

1953

	The *Grenzpolizei* are increased to 35,000 men.
17 June	The East Berlin Uprising: workers protest against increased work quotas, and are suppressed by the Soviet Army; DDR security forces not involved.
14 November	The Western Powers drop the Interzonal Passes, but East Germans need permission to travel to the West.

1955

| 5 May | Full sovereignty is granted to the BRD. |
| 12 November | The *Bundeswehr* is established. |

1956

| 1 March | The *Nationale Volksarmee* is established. |

1957

| 11 December | An illegal frontier crossing statute (*Grenzgesetz*) is enacted by the DDR. Violations are prosecuted with up to three years in prison. |

1960

| 8 September | Visa restrictions are imposed by the DDR. |

1961

13 August	The Berlin Wall is erected and the DDR/BRD border closed.
14 August	The Brandenburg Gate is closed.
23 August	East Berlin is closed to West Berliners.
24 August	The first East Berliner is killed trying to escape.
15 September	The *Grenzpolizei* are reorganized as *Grenztruppen der NVA*.
27–28 October	A stand-off develops between US and Soviet tanks at Checkpoint Charlie in Berlin.

1962

| 19 June | The IGB security zone is established with a second inner fence. |

1963

26 June	US President John F. Kennedy gives his '*Ich bin ein Berliner*' ('I am a Berliner') speech in West Berlin.
17 December	West Berliners may now visit East Berlin.

1971

3 September	The Four Power Agreement over Berlin is signed, whereby visits to the East are made easier for West Berliners.
17 December	Transit agreement is signed between the BRD and DDR.

1972

21 December	The Basis of Relations Treaty is signed, in which the BRD recognizes the DDR as a sovereign nation.

1973

21 June	BRD residents near the frontier are allowed to obtain visas to visit relatives in the DDR.

1974

28 February	The *Grenztruppen* are transferred from the NVA to the *Ministerium des Innern* (MdI – the Ministry of the Interior).

1977

7 October	East Berlin youths protest against the Wall, and are suppressed by the *Volkspolizei* (Vopo – People's Police).

1987

12 June	President Ronald Reagan visits Berlin and invites Soviet President Mikhail Gorbachev to 'tear down this wall'.

1989

5 February	The last escapee to be shot crossing the Wall is killed.
8 April	The last escape attempt from East Berlin takes place, and is stopped by gunfire.
Summer	Widespread protests across the DDR take place, demanding free elections and freedom of travel.
10 September	The Hungarian government opens its border to East German refugees, who can then travel to Austria and on to the BRD.
17 October	Erich Honecker is replaced as the DDR leader.
9 November	The Berlin Wall is opened.
22 December	The Brandenburg Gate is opened.

1990

18 March	The Unification Treaty between the BRD and DDR is signed.
31 May	Stasi and NVA intelligence agents in the BRD are ordered to 'come in from the cold'.
30 June	Following pressure by citizens, all frontier controls are dissolved.
1 July	The *Grenztruppen* are dissolved.
31 August	Treaty on the Establishment of a Unified Germany is signed.
23 September	The Unification Treaty Act is passed.
3 October	Germany and Berlin are reunited.

A pair of East German Frontier Police patrol the frontier. Asphalt was torn up to make the control strip continuous. A patrol footpath edged the 'death strip'. Here, vertical barbed-wire ties prevent the horizontal strands from being spread apart.

A collection of BRD frontier warning and marking signs at the Grenzland Museum, Eichsfeld. The forest-green hut is typical of those found controlling checkpoint entries to the frontier's restricted zone on the DDR side. (Glenn Allardyce)

These black, red and gold *Grenzsäule* (up to 1.6m in height) were placed at 450–480m intervals and 5m from the actual border. The silvery metal DDR *Staateemblem* faced the BRD side. On the back was the post number in black. The top was a blunt pyramid with a protruding short iron rod to discourage birds from perching. (Glenn Allardyce)

THE INTRA-GERMAN BORDER

In early 1952 the USSR had become concerned with the supposed 'infiltration of Western agents and saboteurs' and the ceaseless exodus of professionals and skilled workers from the DDR. In April a meeting was held between Stalin and the DDR leaders. The Soviet foreign minister, Vyacheslav Molotov, proposed that the DDR should implement a pass system for Westerners visiting East Berlin, to impede Western agents. Stalin took this a step further and recommended that the entire demarcation line between East and West Germany now be considered a border, and closed to prevent movement in either direction. Less than two months later this was implemented. 'Flight from the republic' (*Republikflucht*) was declared illegal.

The border 1952–67

The IGB, or what the Germans simply called *die Grenze* (the Frontier), ran from the Baltic Sea to the Czechoslovak border for 1,381km.[1] In some places it followed former Reich administrative boundaries. In other places it deviated, having been negotiated by American, British and French occupation officers with the Soviets. In 1955 the security of the IGB became the responsibility of the

---

1 The IGB's length varied depending on the sources consulted. The US Army said 1,345.9km, the British Army of the Rhine 1,393km, and the BRD 1,381km, which is the measurement used in this work.

A   A TYPICAL SECTION OF THE INTRA-GERMAN BORDER IN THE 1950s

1. Actual BRD/DDR border.
2. 1.2–2.5m-high barbed-wire fence.
3. 4–13m-wide control strip.
4. Patrol path.
5. Wooden guard tower.
6. Fixed gate pole.
7. Frontier warning sign 'Halt! Hier Grenze'.
8. Anti-vehicle ditch and earth berm.
9. Barbed-wire-wrapped anti-vehicle posts.
10. Trees cleared between border and fence.
11. Concrete observation bunker.
12. Barbed-wire and steel grating blocking stream.
13. Patrol path footbridge.
14. Frontier patrol (*Grenzposten*) on foot.

A typical section of the Intra-German Border in the 1950s

15

DDR. While not as well known as the Wall, the IGB was the true frontline between NATO forces and the Warsaw Pact for the 50 years of the Cold War. It cut villages in two (even running though buildings), separated towns from their churches, cemeteries and hospitals, and denied farmers access to their fields and local producers their markets. In short, it fundamentally changed society. Extended families found themselves living in different countries separated sometimes by only metres, but unable to visit each other. A common scene on the frontier was a family with their children waving to grandparents on the other side under the stern watchfulness of DDR *Grenztruppen*. All autobahns, roads, trails, railways, and canals were cut except for specified routes to West Berlin.

When the border between the DDR and BRD was closed on 26 May 1952, the frontier barriers were to all intents and purposes symbolic, and were inadequate for preventing escape. However, the closure did cut commercial and private movement between the two countries. Three autobahns, 30 main roads, 66 major roads, some 70 secondary roads, 35 out of 43 railway lines, and thousands of local roads, village streets, private roads and country lanes were closed, as were river and canal routes.

Regardless of rhetoric claiming the frontier was to defend against Western aggression, the barriers were clearly intended to imprison East Germany's population. They had no military value, were not intended as obstacles to any imagined NATO invasion, and were not designed to slow and canalize an attacking army. It was at this time that the frontier security regime (*Grenzsicherungsregime*) with a 5km-wide restricted zone was established along with a 500m-wide security zone, into which only authorized persons were allowed. In May and June 1952 several thousand 'dangerous persons' were relocated from the restricted zone during Action Vermin (*Aktion Ungesiefer*). The similar Action Cornflower (*Aktion Kornblume*) was executed in 1961 after the Berlin Wall was erected. Some 12,000 people were relocated in both operations.

There was no standardization of the barriers or control strip, as farmers were initially ordered to plough them into their land. The frontier fences were installed gradually, first by the Soviets and then by the East Germans, with remote sectors far away from villages and access roads being the lowest priority. The barriers were usually just inside the actual border, although in some sectors they were set back from the border. Barbed-wire fences (*Stacheldrahtzäune*) were 1.2–1.5m high, but could be as much as 2.5m high, on square or round posts with 12–20 strands of barbed wire (*Stacheldraht*). Sometimes, the lower strands were more closely spaced to hamper escapees crawling through. Vertical barbed-wire strands were sometimes twisted through the horizontal stands at one-metre intervals to prevent them from being spread. In some sectors fences were so poorly constructed or maintained that livestock could wander through. Vegetation was cleared along the fence courses, but was often left adjacent to fences, as there was simply not the manpower to do this.

The frontier fence ran across autobahns, roads and railway tracks, but sometimes a gap was left, with the red and white-banded gate poles lowered and the route closed by chevaux-de-frise barricades. A metal or wooden white disc with a red border might be attached to the gate pole. Some roads had barbed wire-wrapped, anti-vehicle posts driven into them, or had ditches across them, with the spoil piled on the west side. Mounds of earth and broken asphalt might be piled on the end of a cut road just inside the border. The bridges crossing rivers and streams on the border were dismantled, or at least had sections removed; even elevated autobahn sections were pulled down.

Railway track sections were pulled up and sometimes a buffer stop (bumper), built of sleepers (crossties), blocked the dead end; derailers were sometimes installed. Often, though, the track merely came to an abrupt dead end. Streams were blocked by fences or grates, which had to be replaced after flooding.

High board fences (*Holzlattenzaun*) were erected on the sides of villages facing the frontier. House windows facing the border were bricked or boarded up, and buildings too close to the border were torn down. There were even instances when the border was declared to bisect houses; they were subsequently bricked up inside on the East German side, or the east portion of the house was simply demolished and a fence erected. In some cases, all or part of small villages were evacuated and levelled; all that remains today are foundation stones and overgrown cemeteries.

Regardless of the type of barrier, a fixture running the entire length of the frontier was the control strip, known as the *Pieck Straße*; it was named after William Pieck, the DDR's (first) president from 1949 to 1960. This graded strip of bare earth was key to the frontier barrier, and was a proven technique inherited from Soviet border troops. It was 4–13m wide and ran parallel with and inside the main fence. A foot patrol path typically ran along the edge opposite the fence; at this time, few patrol roads ran parallel to the fence. The control strip ran across cut autobahns and roads, with their concrete or asphalt pulled up. It paralleled streams and rivers on the DDR side. The strip is usually described as being ploughed, but in reality it was actually harrowed.[2] After rains or heavy winds, or if weeds grew, the strip was freshly harrowed to re-loosen it, thus making footprints more visible. The control strip did little to prevent escape attempts unless it was kept under constant observation – a basic principle of obstacle employment. Its value was as a means of determining how many escapees had crossed, in what areas escapes were successful, and the times of day when crossings were being made (between patrols). This alerted the *Grenzpolizei* as to when and where patrols needed to be increased, and where guard towers should be installed and fencing reinforced.

The early guard towers (*Wachturn*) were erected only in small numbers in high-traffic areas. They were of simple, non-standard design, comprising a rectangular or square board hut with a small window in each side perched atop locally cut timber legs. Some more elaborate towers had a railed catwalk around the outside. Access was via a ladder and floor hatch. Small ground-level plank observation huts were also used.

There were only a few thousand *Grenzpolizist* to cover the porous border and man legal crossing points. They were stretched to the limit and poorly trained. Their quarters were Spartan, being former Wehrmacht barracks, vacated houses, huts or tents.

The IGB's southern end did not tie into the Czechoslovak frontier barriers. Instead, the fence and control strip turned east and continued to run along the Soviet Zone's southern border, to be faced with a similar fence on the Czechoslovak side secured by the *Pohrani ní Stráž* (Border Guard). On the frontier's northern end, a staked-down line of end-to-end chevaux-de-frise ran across the Baltic Sea beach at Priwall. These had to be replaced after storms washed them away. The east side of the beach was a restricted area and was fenced off from the hinterland for a considerable distance, to prevent swimmers and people in small boats from escaping.

DDR anti-personnel mines		
Mine	Origin	Years emplaced
POMS-2/2M	USSR	1961–70
PMD-6M	USSR	1962–79
PMN-2	USSR/ Bulgaria	1963–85
PMP-71	DDR	1971–85
PPM-2	DDR	1971–85

---

2 A harrow was a rectangular steel frame with short steel-rod teeth that was dragged by a team of horses to rake the ground and loosen the soil.

In the late 1950s what could be termed the second-generation barriers began to be emplaced in key sectors, namely those with a high escape rate. These consisted of 15cm-square, 2m-high reinforced concrete posts set at 3m intervals. They were set in two parallel rows 2–10m apart. Nine to twelve strands of barbed wire were attached to both fences. In high-traffic areas, coils of concertina wire were placed between the fences. Short wooden anchor posts were placed about 2m outwards from both fences, with a row running along in between the two. Stakes were aligned between each pair of concrete posts, and anchor wires (double-twisted barbed wire) were tautly stretched from the tops of the concrete posts to the anchor stakes in a V shape. In low-risk sectors only a single fence may have been erected. The fence was often built very close to the actual border. With the increase in *Grenzpolizei* strength, more towers were installed. Dirt patrol tracks, allowing vehicle travel, appeared in some areas, although during and after rain many of these tracks became impassable.

In many areas anti-personnel landmines were planted between the double fences. Some 1.3 million mines of all types were installed from 1961 in 555km of minefields. A standard minefield was 23 × 180m with mines laid in three rows. The most common was the Soviet PMD-6M 'wooden box' or 'shoebox' mine. The only metal component was the small firing device, making it difficult to detect with mine detectors. Being wood and unsealed, the mines deteriorated rapidly, but could remain dangerous for years. They were often washed out by rains and into farmers' fields, and could travel considerable distances down

A portion of the 3m-high expanded-steel mesh frontier fence on concrete posts at 3m intervals. To the right is a damaged section that has been roughly repaired. (Glenn Allardyce)

A section of the electronic signal fence at the Grenzland Museum. The yellow plastic insulators can be seen on the vertical support posts and the Y-shaped outriggers. These were not electrified to be deadly, rather they were merely motion sensors. Note the cut ends of the top edge of the expanded-mesh fence. (Glenn Allardyce)

streams both west and east. They were dangerous to *Grenzpionieren* repairing barriers as well, especially since their locations were poorly recorded. Later, more durable PMN-2, PMP-71 and PPM-2 plastic mines were introduced. These mines had to be stepped on to detonate, with the exception of the POMS-2 stake mine, which was tripwire activated. There were no mine warnings on the DDR side, but *Achtung Minen!* was often posted by the BRD on its side.

The mines began to be removed in 1976 when the new, expanded-steel mesh fences were erected with tripwire-activated SM-71 mines fitted to these. Some of the old PMD-6M and new plastic mines were laid in 1976 owing to problems with SM-70s being detonated by rain and snow. In 1985 the DDR reported that all mines had been removed, but after reunification it was discovered that a poor job had been done of it.

In contrast, on the West German side of the frontier there were no barriers of any kind. The West Germans did not even establish patrol roads on their side. There were only some frontier signs (*Grenzschilder*) warning *Achtung!*

BOTTOM LEFT
Reinforced-concrete patrol road segments. Each segment was pierced by four rows of seven rectangular holes. (Glenn Allardyce)

BOTTOM RIGHT
From left to right: the expanded-mesh frontier fence, a grass trip, the control strip, another grass strip and the patrol road. (Glenn Allardyce)

A 1.2 × 1.5m, 15cm-thick reinforced-concrete anti-vehicle slab. These lined the side of the ditch facing into the DDR. They were normally set at an almost vertical angle. The large panel on the fence is a tourist guide sign. (Glenn Allardyce)

Zonengrenze (Attention! Zonal Frontier) or *Halt! Hier Grenze* (Halt! This is the Frontier). Interspaced between the signs were 2m-high, 80mm-diameter white pipes with red (or blue in Bavaria) tops (*Grenzpfosten*), for identifying the border even in heavy snow. The West Germans usually erected a red and white-striped horizontal pole across roads mounted on two white posts. Foreign military personnel were restricted from approaching the frontier unless on official duty. West Germans were free to approach the border, and school tours and families trips to see the *Grenz* were common.

The actual border was marked by 200mm-square granite blocks (*Grenzsteinen*) marked with a '+' on top and DDR on the west side; these were placed at irregular intervals and at angular changes. The actual border alignment was agreed on by the joint *Grenz-Kommission*. In August 1967 the DDR erected 2,622 1.5–1.6m-high, square, concrete posts at 450–480m intervals approximately 5m inside the border. The markers (*Grenzsäule* or *Grenzpfahl*, 'barber poles') were diagonally banded black, red and gold with a cast metal DDR coat of arms (*Staateemblem*) affixed to the top facing the BRD.

The West Germans did patrol and observe the frontier, mainly for customs purposes, to prevent and report border violations by the DDR, and to prevent BRD citizens from tampering with and defacing DDR border markers, which led to DDR protests. The BRD authorities involved with the frontier were the *Bundesgrenzschutz* (Federal Frontier Protection), *Bayerische Grenzpolizei* (Bavarian Frontier Police) and *Bundeszollverwaltung* (Federal Customs Administration).

The modern border 1968–98

The frontier barriers proved to be only marginally effective in halting escapes. An escapee, especially one displaying determination and imagination and fortunate enough to make his attempt between passing patrols, had little trouble traversing the barriers in most areas. By now the *Grenztruppen* was a significantly larger, better-trained force, and had absorbed a great deal. The decision was made to develop a modern border system designed to drastically reduce escapes. Many of the barrier, detection and surveillance means so successfully used in Berlin would be incorporated into the new system. Instead of barbed wire, difficult-to-climb steel mesh fencing would be used, and directional anti-personnel mines, anti-vehicle ditches, inner barrier fences with electronic movement detectors, an all-weather patrol road, concrete guard towers and low-profile observation bunkers would be created. It was hoped that this third-generation border would provide a more escape-proof system, would be less demanding on manpower, and would present a less intimidating and negative appearance to Western and world observers. Construction of the third-generation border (or the 'modern frontier') began in September 1967 and was originally to have been completed in 1970. This carried over into 1972 owing to bureaucratic inefficiency and financial shortfalls, and improvements continued into the 1980s. A total of 1,289km of new fencing (excluding double-fences and the inner electronic fence of almost the same length) lined the new border.

The third-generation border retained the 5km restricted zone, wider or narrower in some areas, running the entire length of the border. This required a considerable area, approximately 6,900km², although portions of it

SM-70 fragmentation mine

In 1970 SM-70 tripwire-activated, directional, anti-personnel mines (*Splittermine 1970*) began to be emplaced on IGB fences, but not on the Berlin Wall. These were often incorrectly called 'automatic firing devices', giving the false impression that they were a type of gun. The mine consisted of a cone filled with 110g of TNT, lined with approximately 110 steel cube fragments, and fitted with an N-172 firing device that was activated by pulling or cutting the tripwire. The assembly was fitted to a bolt-on mounting bracket attached to concrete fence posts. One mine was attached to a post near the ground, a second mine was attached midway up the next post, and a third on another post near the top of the fencing. The cones were aimed to the left (on the east side) parallel with the fence. The three mines' horizontal tripwires ran tautly, by-passing the following few posts and then being anchored to the mounting brackets of the next set of three mines. Anti-bird wires protected the tripwires from accidental detonations, with one running above each tripwire and another fitted to an outrigger level with the tripwire. Nonetheless, birds managed to set them off occasionally, as did deer, boars, other wildlife, heavy rains and wind, falling tree branches, deep snow and West German pranksters hurling stones. To better protect them from the elements, they were soon encased in two-piece, 115mm-square, 55mm-thick grey plastic boxes. Some 60,000 were emplaced on 440km of escape-prone sectors. They were lethal up to a range of 120m, as attested by the bodies of dead deer. The first two SM-70s to fall into the

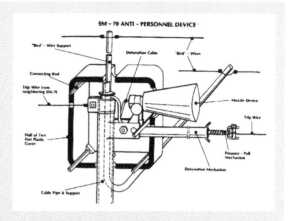

hands of the BRD authorities were stolen off the fence by a former DDR citizen (who had served 10 years' imprisonment for agitation before being released to the BRD). He was ambushed and killed by *Grenztruppen* during a second attempt. The DDR had denied the existence of the mines even though they were clearly present. International pressure forced the DDR to remove the mines, and the last was dismantled on 30 November 1984. It is rumoured that the SM-70 was developed from a World War II SS prototype intended for concentration camps.

were still used for grazing and agriculture, and contained some villages. For comparison, today's reunited Berlin covers 890km², Greater London 1,706km², and Los Angeles 1,215km². Together these three major cities would fill just over half of the land occupied by the restricted zone, a considerable sacrifice for a country slightly smaller than the state of Kentucky, but with over four times the population.

Descriptions of the modern frontier system are usually from the Western perspective looking into the DDR, but for the purposes of this work we will discuss it from the viewpoint of an escapee travelling to the West. It should be noted that the terms 'west' and 'east' are convenient generalities. The border twisted and turned along its length, following terrain features and rivers, and with bulges and cul-de-sacs all along. One could conceivably escape north, south and even east.

An SM-70 anti-personnel mine with the anti-bird wires rigged; however, it lacks the firing device wire. (Glenn Allardyce)

The Vopos and other security organs were more active the closer one approached to the restricted zone (*Sperrzone*) and loyal citizens were alert for strangers and unfamiliar vehicles. Controls were strict for citizens living or working in the zone. It was almost impossible for friends or families to visit. Residents had special vehicle tags and identity cards. If a farmer were to work his fields inside the zone he had to report to the *Grenztruppen* garrison in advance and complete a request form with entry and departure times, his purpose, and so on. There were instances of family members being left behind with the border garrison, to idle away a non-productive day.

Frontier surveillance complex, Pötenitz

22

The restricted zone was not fenced, but marked with conspicuous warning signs. Control checkpoints (*Kontrollpassierpunkt*) were situated on the entry roads. The electronic sensor fence (*Signalzaun*) or 'hinterland fence' might be 500–1,000m from the border. It served as the boundary of the security zone (*Schultzzone*) and had control posts at the entrances. It had a 2m-wide control strip on its east side. Where possible, it followed the contour of high ground and ran through open areas. This made it more observable from different vantage points and intruders were silhouetted against the sky. The *Signalzaun* was a 2m-high, expanded-steel mesh fence with the mesh panels fastened to the west side. Strung on the east side were 16 horizontal, barbed-wire strands at 15cm intervals attached to insulators on every post. If they were cut, or if two were touched at the same time, signal alarms were set off in the control towers. On the post tops were Y-shaped outriggers with four barbed-wire strands on each arm running through insulators. There were also two plain sensor wires on angled, half-metre outrigger rods near the bottom and midway up. The outriggers were attached to every second or third post. These also set off alarms if touched. In 1973, after the signal fence was installed, the entry points on the 5km restricted zone were closed, although the area was still patrolled. By mid-1974 it was discovered that the fences malfunctioned so frequently they could not be relied on.

A cut-away mock-up of an SM-70 anti-personnel mine displaying the explosive- and fragmentation-filled cone and the N-172 pull/tension-release firing device. The two prongs were to support anti-bird wires. The detail of the expanded-steel mesh fencing can be seen here. (Glenn Allardyce)

Inside the security zone there were often wide, clear areas comprising pasture and cultivated fields, but much of it was forested or brush-covered. Towers and concrete bunkers were sited at vantage points providing maximum fields of observation and fire. Minefields, where installed, were often set back from the main outer fence and might be situated between two mesh or barbed-wire fences about 25m apart.

The patrol road (*Kolonnenweg*) ran roughly parallel to the main fence, fairly close to the control strip, so that it and the fence could be easily examined. The improved, one-way, all-weather road carried vehicle and foot traffic. It consisted of approximately 0.75m-wide, 2.5m-long, 200cm-thick reinforced-concrete slabs laid end to end in two parallel lines. The blocks were pierced with four rows of seven rectangular holes. They were set flush with the ground. Sometimes they were laid crosswise as a continuous roadway. They were also used for other construction projects, such as foundations for towers and revetting embankments and mounds on which towers were built.

Anti-vehicular ditches (*Kraftfahrzeug Sperrgraben*) could be present on either side of the patrol road depending on the terrain and cross-country vehicle approaches. Approximately two-thirds of the border was protected by such ditches; the remaining third was covered by dense forests, rivers, lakes, drainage ditches, irrigation canals, gullies and steep-banked streams. The anti-vehicle ditch was a V-shaped cut with the east entry slope being shallow and the west side slanted at a steep angle; it was faced with 1.2m x 1.5m,

The northern terminus of the IGB on the Baltic coast was adjacent to Priwall, BRD and near Pötenitz, DDR. The frontier cut across the east base of the Priwall Peninsula and followed the west shore of the Pötenitzer Wiek, a bay-like inlet of the River Trave. The surveillance complex overlooked the beach and inshore waters some 250m from the border. There were no barriers blocking the beach, but fences and anti-vehicle ditches were emplaced further inland from the complex. The BRD set a line of chest-high, steel

T-pipe posts down to the low-tide line linked with heavy chain, the chain and posts banded red and white (1). A line of white marker buoys (2) stretched a few hundred metres into the sea. The fenced complex included a BT-9 tower (3), observation platform (4), concrete bunker (5) and perimeter floodlights, with large spotlights (6) illuminating the beach and water. A BT-11 tower (7) had been emplaced prior to the BT-9. On the BRD side (8) there was nothing other than a beach resort area, which included a nudist beach.

The IGB in the 1980s, as portrayed by an instructional flyer issued by the BRD Federal Frontier Police.

1. BRD frontier warning sign: 'Achtung! Nach 100m Grenze'.
2. BRD red and white frontier marker post with warning sign: 'Halt! Hier Grenze'.
3. DDR frontier stones marking the actual border.
4. BRD red and white frontier marker post.
5. DDR black, red and gold frontier columns.
6. Clear-cut strip of DDR territory outside the fence.
7. Double expanded-steel mesh fence, possibly with landmines between.
8. Single expanded-steel mesh fence with SM-70 anti-personnel mines on the posts.
9. Concrete, slab-faced anti-vehicle ditch.
10. 6m-wide control strip.
11. Concrete slab patrol road.
12. BT-9 guard tower.
13. BT-11 guard tower.
14. Concrete observation bunker.
15. Floodlight poles.
16. Telephone checkpoint box.
17. Dog run with doghouse.
18. Security zone entry checkpoint.
19. Concrete barrier wall surrounding a village.
20. Hinterland electronic detection fence.
21. Double steel gates accessing the exterior frontier strip.

15cm-thick reinforced-concrete slabs. The ditches were at least 80cm deep and would stop just about anything: the East Germans tried with cars, farm trucks, tractors, and even bulldozers to break through the frontier barriers.

Another anti-vehicle obstacle was the *Panzersperre*, the steel hedgehog or *Stahligeln*. These were made of three or four pairs of 1.5m-long rail tracks. Two lengths of rail were welded side by side, one with the head (top edge) up and the other down. Three pairs were welded to form a tripod and the fourth section (not always present) was welded between two of the legs. At over 545kg it was heavy enough to prevent a car from pushing it out of the way. Although more common on the Berlin Wall, they were used on the IGB.

The standard control strip paralleled the fence abutting it. It was generally 6m wide although wider sections were recorded. The 'death strip' (*Todesstreifen*) was so-called because an individual entering the strip could be shot, after a warning had been given. The *Grenzer* called it the 'action strip' (*Handlungsstreifen*). Rather than requiring farmers to harrow the strip, *Grenzpionieren* now did it using 3m-wide harrows towed by KT-50 bulldozers (*Raupenschlepper*).

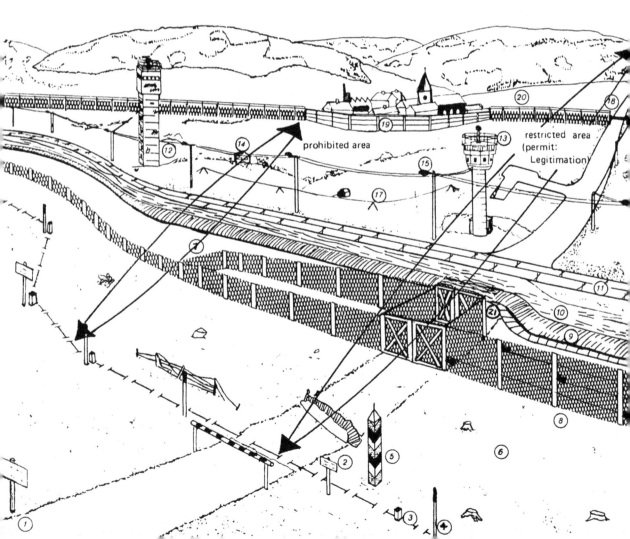

prohibited area

restricted area
(permit:
Legitimation)

The main fence was formidable, even though it looked less intimidating than tangled barbed wire. The standard fence was 3.2–4m high and bolted to 15cm-square, reinforced concrete posts set at 2m intervals. The posts were on the outer (west) side of the mesh to prevent escapees climbing up them. The galvanized, expanded-steel mesh fence (*Metallgitterzaun*) panels, measuring 1m × 3m, were made from heavy-gauge steel in a diamond-shaped pattern; the openings varied in size and were either 12 × 45mm or 20 × 75mm. The smaller of the two openings were barely large enough for bare fingers to fit into (let alone gloved ones), and were very sharp. Unlike the larger mesh areas, the smaller of hardened mesh could not be cut through with a bolt- or wire-cutter, only with an acetylene torch. When attached to the posts the panels overlapped by 3–8cm and were fastened by rivets and washers. There was a hole in the post near the top and three pairs of holes down its length to take the mesh attachment bolts. For 4m-high fences, four horizontal mesh panels were used with about half of the lower panel buried in the ground; the 3.2m-high fences had three panels with a fourth overlapping the bottom and half buried in the ground. There were also various types of lighter barriers (*Lichtsperren*), which were simple mesh and barbed-wire fences. Somewhat surprisingly, the mesh fencing was manufactured in the BRD.

The detail of the SM-70 post mounting bracket can be seen here. Note too the bolt hole on the west side of the white-painted post. The bolt had a large flat washer on the opposite side.

Gates (*Durchlass*) through the fence were constructed of square steel tubes and flat stock frameworks and attached to 14cm-diameter steel posts by heavy-duty hinges. The hinges were on the outside and the pivot pins were welded to prevent removal. The gates opened inward and were chained and locked with heavy-duty padlocks. A saw-tooth steel strip was welded across the top bar.

In some areas there were two parallel fences 10–20m apart. Often a double-fenced area was created; there was a gate to the outer strip, meaning that two gates had to be passed through. The fences were seldom topped by barbed wire, but sometimes Y-shaped outriggers supported three strands of wire on both sides.

The sides of villages abutting or near the border were faced with 3–4m-high concrete barrier walls (*Betonsperrmauern*). One example was at Mödlareuth in Bavaria, dubbed 'Little Berlin' by the Americans. In 1966 a 3.4m-high, 700m-long concrete wall was erected; previously there had been a barbed-wire fence. The wall may have been topped with barbed wire or sewer pipes. In some instances large-diameter steel pipes were mounted horizontally on brackets atop walls. An escapee grasping the pipe would find that it rolled; however, the pipes could be jammed still with wooden wedges or pieces of concrete, and so were not widely used. High-intensity floodlights (*Beleuch-tungsanlage*) were installed atop concrete poles along the patrol road to illuminate the control strip and fence in vulnerable areas (the walls around villages were also often illuminated, as were rivers and streams crossing the border).

A typical early guard tower was a simple hut on 4m-long, locally cut timber legs. Similar towers up to 7m high were also used.

Another means of hindering escapes was to emplace dog runs (*Hundefreilungs*). Steel cables up to 100m long were suspended above the ground on steel bipods (tripods at the ends) with a doghouse. A watchdog was clipped to the cable with a cable leash. The runs were portable so that they could be installed where necessary. Sometimes temporary pens were installed adjacent to border fence gates or a damaged fence portion awaiting repair. To access the gate one had to enter the pen. A dog might also be released in short sections of double fences at gates.

When the third-generation fence began to be emplaced, it was generally built east of the earlier fence. Once the new barriers had been installed, the old fencing was removed, although remnants were left in some areas. This

RIGHT
A BT-9 observation tower mounting a searchlight and radio antenna. (Glenn Allardyce)

FAR RIGHT
A 30cm, 1,000-watt searchlight (*Suchscheinwerfer*) on a portable ground mounting. Similar lights were mounted atop guard towers. This one is forest green, but those mounted on towers were usually light grey. (Glenn Allardyce)

provided a 20–100m-wide (though up to 2km in some areas) section of no-man's land. It provided a clear field of fire for engaging escapees that had made it over the fence, and access for fence repairs and mowing the grass, and for *Grenzaufklärungstruppen* to venture out for intelligence collection. Areas where the outer strip was very wide was where escape attempts were most likely, as there were seldom any obstacles in this strip other than earth mounds or ditches across the end of cut roads.

Towers

There were three types of guard towers (*Watchturm*), which replaced the flimsy, locally built wooden towers. Towers were not set at any particular intervals or distance from the border. They were situated where they provided the best observation. Some were semi-portable and could be repositioned. The *Grenzpionieren* possessed truck-mounted cranes, tractors, and heavy transport trailers to move tower and bunker sections and erect them.

The first type met three *Grenztruppen* requirements, namely that it should be low cost, semi-portable, and rapidly erected, and was called the BT-11 observation tower (*Beobachtungtrum 11-metre*). The Grenztruppen called it a panoramic observation tower (*Rundblickbeobachtungsturm*, or RBT); they were introduced in 1969. A concrete foundation was poured, 11 interlocking 1m-thick circular concrete sections were stacked, and the observation compartment hoisted by crane to crown it. There was a door in the columns' two bottom sections facing away from the border that could only be locked from the inside. A steel pipe ladder allowed access to the top of the compartment. The eight-sided reinforced concrete compartment had windows all around with a firing port in the lower side-walls. The windows could also be opened upward. On the bluntly conical roof was a 30cm 1,000-watt searchlight (*Suchscheinwerfer*) that could be aimed from the inside. The roof was surrounded by a safety rail for servicing the light, and had an access hatch. Two lightning-conductor cables ran from the roof down the column to the ground.

This illustration shows three different types of guard tower. (1) BT-11 (*Beobachtungtrum 11-metre*) tower. The support column has a diameter of 1m, and the tower consists of 11 pre-fabricated concrete sections excluding the observation compartment on top. (2) BT-9 (*Beobachtungtrum 9-metre*) tower. The support column consists of nine 2 × 2m square concrete blocks placed on top of each other, totalling 9m in height (excludes the observation compartment). The firing ports, one on each side, are located in the penultimate concrete section below the observation compartment, which measures 2.3 × 2.3m and is topped with a radio antenna. (3) Observation and command station (*Führungsstelle*) – also known as a *Kommandoturm*. The support column consists of four 4 × 4m sections of concrete, and this is topped with a 2m-high observation compartment. The tower has a total height of 6m, and the sides feature vents as well as firing ports. Note the air intake box at ground level.

While the DDR erected hundreds of guard towers on their side of the IGB, the Americans maintained fewer than a dozen permanent observation posts. An M59 armoured personnel carrier can be seen to the rear of this photo taken in the early 1960s.

The tower was connected to power and telephone lines. There were instances of one or two sections of the observation tower column being erected atop a mound, and entered through a hatch and tunnel in the mound's rear. Some were shorter, usually in towns or restricted areas where elevation did not improve observation. If it was determined that a sector had to be reinforced, a BT-11 could be erected in a few days. Being top heavy, with a large slab-sided compartment atop a narrow flimsy column, problems were encountered: the towers could collapse in extremely high winds or if heavy rain had softened the ground around the foundations.

In the mid-1970s a more permanent and stable guard tower was introduced, the BT-9. This was a 9m-high square tower, measuring 2×2m in cross-section. The base section was 2m high with a door set in one wall. Beside the door was a concrete box containing the air intake system. Six 1m sections were stacked atop the base. There was a firing port in each side of the fifth segment. The four-sided 2.3×2.3m observation compartment was set on top. It had four recessed windows on all sides, which could be opened for firing, a safety rail on top with a hatch, and a 30cm searchlight. The BT-9 towers were built in areas where permanent surveillance was necessary.

A third type of tower doubled as an observation and command station (*Führungsstelle* – a.k.a. *Kommandoturm*) and was the least common. It measured 4×4m with four 1m sections topped by a 2m-high compartment, for an overall height of 6m. It was often built on a 1m earth or concrete foundation. The third section up had two firing ports on each side, the section below it may have had three air vents, and the one below that perhaps one vent. The internal stairs lacked railings. The observation compartment had four windows in each side. The roof arrangement was as per the BT-9.

Command towers contained various controls: signal fence controls and alert lights, SM-70 mine detonation indicators, controls for remotely lowering border crossing gates, searchlight controls, fence lighting controls, and a telephone connected to other towers, guard posts, patrol telephone checkpoints, and the unit *Kaserne*. There was also a Frontier Information Point telephone connected to the BRD *Bundesgrenzschutz* across the border. They stiffly exchanged a formatted report to one another at 8 a.m. each day on any incidents occurring the preceding night, to prevent misunderstandings. There were long-range antennas for R-105 radios on the roof. The battalion and regimental command towers had three or four radios. The older type – usually 8m-high, wooden or steel towers – remained in limited use, along with little-used observation platforms in trees.

Much less common were the small, semi-portable, reinforced concrete bunkers known as 'earth bunkers' (*Erdbunker*). They were usually partly buried below ground, but were sometimes set on a ground-level concrete slab. They had two 0.8m-high, stacked 1.6×1.6m base sections with a small wooden door in the back. The third, top section had two steel-shuttered firing ports in the front and one in each of the other three sides. Some had two ports in the sides. The bluntly pointed roof was a separate nesting component. The bunkers were used as observation posts. There were older bunkers of masonry or poured concrete construction, usually with fewer ports.

The barriers and facilities securing the IGB made it the second most heavily fortified border in the world, the first being the Demilitarized Zone of Korea. In mid-1989 the IGB consisted of:

Expanded-steel mesh fencing	1,265km
Hinterland signal fencing	1,185km
Concrete barrier walls	29.1km
Anti-vehicle ditches	829km
Light barbed-wire barriers	232.3km
Dog runs	71.5km
Patrol roads	1,339.1km
Concrete observation towers	529
Steel and wood observation towers	155
Observation bunkers	425

The modern frontier proved to be very effective. In the last half of the 1960s an average of 500 successful escapes were made each year. In 1970, before the new border barriers were even completed, this had dropped to 25.

THE BERLIN WALL

Two months before the Berlin Wall was built, President Walter Ulbricht of the DDR declared, *'Niemand hat die Absicht, eine Mauer zu errichten!'* ('No one intends to set up a wall!'); it was the first time the colloquial term *Mauer* (Wall) was used in this context. To prevent the increasing migration to the West, Ulbricht proposed a second Berlin blockade. Although the border between East and West Germany had already been sealed, West Berlin provided a last route of escape and illegal money exchange, which was hurting the faltering DDR economy. Khrushchev rejected this proposal, owing to the failure of the first blockade; NATO was now even better equipped for supplying the city by air. Khrushchev approved the plan for the Wall, code-named 'Rose'. It was first to be constructed only of barbed wire, and if NATO troops challenged its construction the East Germans were to fall back without firing. Had the West chosen to intervene in its construction, it might have prevented West Berlin's 30-year isolation. The Wall was built under the direction of Erich Honecker, Secretariat of the Central Committee and from 1971 the DDR's leader.

In the early morning hours of Sunday 13 August 1961, West Berlin was awakened by the sounds of trucks, tractors, cranes, military vehicles, and marching troops. The West was taken entirely by surprise as 20,000 armed troops moved into position surrounding the city beginning at 2 a.m. Kilometres-long columns of vehicles streamed in from all over the DDR. The troops did not know what was happening until they reached their posts. It was a well-planned operation involving much of the East German uniformed forces, the People's Police, Frontier Police and Worker's Militia plus Soviet troops. Even girls of youth organizations served food to the troops and labourers. Construction materials and heavy equipment had also been secretly prepared.

The 155km of West Berlin's city frontier (*Stadtgrenze*) on its north, west and south sides had been closed since 1952. Now, the 43.1km-long

West Berliners peer over the Wall, possibly looking for separated relatives. The use of multiple materials to construct the early walls is apparent.

Checkpoint Charlie

Checkpoint (CP) Charlie was one of several official frontier crossing points between the East and West, a symbol of the Cold War, and a focal point of many spy thrillers. The checkpoints, either between West and East Berlin or on the autobahns entering West Berlin, were named using the NATO Phonetic Alphabet. The West Germans called CP Charlie *Sektorenübergang Friedrichstraße* and the East Germans *Grenzübergangsstelle Friedrich-Zimmerstraße* (after the street intersection). CP Charlie was in the American Sector and restricted to military and diplomatic personnel, who could still enter East Berlin. Other checkpoints served West German citizens. By 1962 it was the only crossing point between East and West Berlin and became the Allied Checkpoint. The actual checkpoint was merely a small light-grey or white-painted wooden booth, two end-to-end huts at one point, over which American and later Allied flags hung. It was situated on a safety island between the traffic lanes. Nearby was a low observation platform. Across the street was the popular Café Adler providing a view of the checkpoint and the East

Berlin side, a site where escape assistants made their plans. To emphasize that the division of Berlin was temporary, the checkpoint was only a temporary structure, although in the 1980s a larger portable metal hut was used. On the east side of the Wall were guard towers, zigzag vehicle barriers, anti-vehicle obstacles, and steel sheds where vehicles were inspected.

The best-known and one of the most dangerous Cold War incidents at CP Charlie was the 27 November 1961 tank stand-off. Vopos were harassing Allied officials entering East Berlin and four M48A1 tanks and two M59 armoured personnel carriers were sent to

CP Charlie to demonstrate American resolve. This time a diplomat was allowed to pass and the US tanks withdrew. As they were doing so, 10 black-painted T-54 tanks appeared, backed by another 23; the crews wore no insignia. American MPs crossed the border and overheard the crews speaking Russian. The outnumbered American tanks returned to face the Soviets at point-blank range. Khrushchev and Kennedy defused the situation the next day and one tank at a time withdrew until Friedrichstraße was clear of belligerent tanks.

CP Charlie was removed in June 1990. The original wooden hut is located at the Allied Museum in Zehlendorf and the later metal hut is now located on the south side of Friedrichstraße at the Museum Haus am Checkpoint Charlie; on the same side of the street is the Maurermuseum. A replica of the checkpoint booth, as it appeared in 1961 complete with its sandbag wall on the east side, now stands in the original location. In July 2005 the bank owning a piece of property leased to the Check Point Charlie Museum removed the 1,067 crosses and a wall section serving as the Memorial for Frontier Dead (*Mahnmal für die Grenztoten*).

A British Royal Military Police NCO on duty at Checkpoint Charlie in West Berlin in October 1964. He is talking to an American and a French military policemen, who are also on duty at the crossing point between West and East Berlin. (IWM TR 23112)

sector frontier (*Sektorengrenze*) separating the two Berlins was being walled off. All except 13 of the 81 official crossing points were closed. In total, 192 streets were cut, 97 into East Berlin and 95 into the DDR.

West Berlin police stations around the city began reporting unusual activity, and the US, British and French occupation forces were alerted. The DDR troops first cordoned off the city and strung concertina wire across streets. Soon they were entering apartments and posting themselves in West-facing windows. All traffic in both directions across the border was halted and DDR Water Protection Police launches patrolled the rivers. The S-Bahn and U-Bahn commuter lines were closed and phone lines were cut. East German radio played only music, with no official announcements. Leaflets were posted announcing the new regulations and handfuls were released to blow into the West. Scores of Soviet T-34 tanks arrived at around 8 a.m. to block key routes. Soon, DDR soldiers began boarding up the Brandenburg Gate (*Brandenburger Tor*), the symbolic gateway to the East. Jackhammers tore up

D BERLIN SPECIAL PURPOSE TOWERS

This illustration shows two types of special purpose towers that were a common sight in Berlin during the Cold War. To the left is a traffic control tower seen on railways and autobahns. The solid support column is topped with a 1.8 × 1.8m observation compartment, which is itself topped with a searchlight. On the side of the compartment are loud speakers. To the right is a less expensive observation tower. It consists of six 1.8 × 1.8m sections of light concrete stacked on top of one another, topped with a sheet-metal observation compartment. It too has a searchlight on top.

paving and cobblestones. Banners and posters went up announcing the *Neu Deutschland* and the efforts to 'protect the East from Western aggression'.

As time went on, thousands of people began lining up on both sides of the border. Western crowds chanted '*KZ, KZ, KZ*', referring to *Konzentrationslager* (concentration camp), and the atmosphere began to sour as the day grew longer. East German and Soviet troops were warned to watch out for saboteurs, and West Berliners were ordered to stay 100m from the line. West Berlin youths began throwing stones and fights with the Vopos broke out. At one point a crowd tore down one of the barriers, and warning shots were fired. The Vopos used spotlights to blind cameras day and night. A record 4,130 refugees escaped to the West that day, 800 after the barricades went up. Eighty-five East German policemen and militiamen bolted in the first six weeks.

Over the following days, more DDR troops were brought in, more wire was strung, and the new border barricades were deepened. The DDR Government proclaimed the Anti-Fascist Protection Wall (*antifaschistische Schutzwall*) was under construction to protect the socialist state. The Berlin Allied commanders (the *Kommandatura*, which the Soviets had dropped out of) protested to the Soviet commander. Hundreds of thousands of West Berliners attended night protest rallies, and targeted some of their anger at the Western Allies' passive response. The USA protested to the Soviets, but could do little as West Berlin itself was under no direct threat and the essentials of the Potsdam Agreement were not being violated – namely the presence of Allied troops, free access to East Berlin by the Western Allies, and the right of self-determination of West Berliners. West Berliners could still enter the East through the remaining entry points using their *ausweis*; many did so, to help get friends and family out, often resorting to bribing the Vopos.

The initial barriers

The first barriers comprised concertina and barbed wire on wooden and concrete posts. At 4 a.m., 1.2m prefab concrete slabs were set by cranes across Ackerstraß, the first street where a wall was actually erected. Ground-floor building windows facing the West were bricked up to prevent escape. However, escapees would use upper windows, dropping notes to the West Berlin police below who would arrange for fire crews to come with nets to catch jumpers. As a result, the upper windows were then bricked up as well. Apartment blocks adjacent to the border were ordered to be vacated on 20 September. This applied to Bernauerstraße in particular, where later all the apartments on the street were torn down and the materials integrated into the Wall. Some buildings were cut in two, with the dividing line bricked up.

The first, expedient walls were low, and made of a variety of different building materials, such as bricks and concrete blocks. These were rapidly replaced with prefab concrete slabs, blocks and beams. The workmanship was crude, with speed being the major concern. Rubble buttresses had to be built to support some sections. Lookout and guard posts began to appear. Steel hedgehog anti-vehicle obstacles were emplaced on streets. Wooden towers began to appear every 1,000m with searchlights sweeping barbed wire, and broken glass was cemented atop the walls. Log and earth lookout bunkers were positioned between the towers. A car driven at speed could crash through these walls in many places, and some of them crumbled after heavy rain as there were no supporting foundations.

West Berliners who aided East Berliners to escape were arrested by the DDR forces when caught. Young men lending identity cards to East Berliners were charged and sentenced to five years' imprisonment for 'organizing the slave trade'. From 23 August 1961 West Berliners were restricted from visiting East Berlin, and the number of authorized crossing points was subsequently reduced to seven. Some East Berliners approved of the Wall, as they deeply resented the professional drain that was taking place. The creation of the Wall was certainly a stabilizing influence in the DDR providing a point of focus and coherence for the Party faithful.

International pressure did little to reverse the situation. It now appeared that Germany could only be reunited by another war. On 2 September the French convinced the East Germans to move the wall back in their sector, as it was 10m inside the French one. The USA called up 75,000 National Guardsmen and reinforced its six divisions in West Germany. On 19 September a column of 500 vehicles and 1,500 US troops crossed from the BRD to West Berlin to ensure right of movement. A battalion was rotated every three months for the next four years, augmenting the Berlin Brigade.

The second- and third-generation walls

The wall that followed immediately on the heels of the initial crude barriers was created using more standardized materials and improved workmanship. Work began on 19 June 1962. Entire blocks of buildings on the border were torn down to create a 30–100m-wide clear area edged by two walls, one on each side. The outer wall was more robust, with continuous improvements made to it, while the inner one was lower. The sandy soil between the two walls was sprayed with defoliants. A 6m-wide, harrowed, control strip paralleled the outer wall and there was an asphalt patrol road. The walls were usually topped by barbed wire, and floodlights were installed on poles. The wire might be affixed

ABOVE LEFT
A *Grenzpioniere* crane truck hoists a concrete slab into position to face an anti-vehicle ditch. These types of truck-mounted cranes were used to emplace concrete fence posts, patrol road slabs, bunker and tower sections, light posts and for other heavy-duty work. (US Army)

ABOVE RIGHT
Here the original fence was left in place when the 'second-generation' wall was built. West Berliners ignored the actual border, which was on the west side of the Wall. This must have been an area where escape attempts were frequent, given the piled mass of concertina wire.

A cross-section of the Berlin Wall security zone in the 1980s

1. Actual BRD/DDR border.
2. 3.6m-high Grenzwall 75 L-shaped wall.
3. Anti-vehicle ditch.
4. Hedgehog anti-vehicle obstacles.
5. 6m-wide control strip.
6. Floodlight poles.
7. Asphalt patrol road.
8. BT-11 guard tower.
9. PSG-80 trip flares.
10. Dog run.
11. Signal alarm equipment, linked to the signal fence.
12. 2m-high signal fence.
13. 3m-high, old-style 'hinterland' wall, topped with barbed wire.

A detailed view of the PSG-80 trip flare on a wire tripod.

to 1m-high vertical steel pickets or Y-shaped pickets with three strands on each angled arm and two on the vertical arm. Anti-vehicle ditches, hedgehogs and embedded concrete blocks were emplaced in vehicle-accessible areas. To reinforce older walls, concrete patrol road sections were stacked on their edges two or three deep and held in place with driven-in steel I-beams. In some areas there was no space for the cleared strip and inner wall, so dense wire entanglements backed the wall and landmines were used. Dog runs were installed and guards often patrolled with attack dogs; some 600 dogs were kept for this purpose. Runs might be the aerial cable type in open areas or 6–7m-wide parallel chain-link fences. More towers were built to cover the new cleared areas and observation posts were concealed in buildings. Guards were under orders not to fire into West Berlin, but this did happen: 456 bullet marks were found on West Berlin walls and paving over the years. As on the IGB, the actual border was outside the outer wall, but usually within only 2–4m – just enough space to allow maintenance crews, who gained access through concealed doors or ladders, to work on the west side. Little effort was made by the *Grenztruppen* to keep West Berliners off this strip, and even pavements ran along it. The walls were whitewashed on the East-facing inside to make it easier to see escapees. On the West side they were whitewashed to cover the perpetually reappearing graffiti: the Wall became a canvas for imaginative political and artistic expression. On 21 June 1963 all East Berliners living within 100m of the security zone had to register with the *Grenztruppen*.

The third-generation wall was begun in 1965 and was a vast improvement over earlier barriers, although it never entirely replaced the previous generation. It consisted of vertical concrete or steel I-beams set in concrete with 15cm-thick, $1 \times 3m$ pre-cast concrete construction panels (*Plattenbauweise*) inserted into the beams' slots, and stacked three (sometimes four and five) high. Approximately 25cm-diameter, thick-walled sewer pipe was fitted to the top on steel mounting brackets, making it impossible to grip on to for climbing over. This feature was incorporated into the Grenzwall 75. In some areas the older, low walls remained outside the new walls, or comprised the primary outer wall. Chain-link and mesh fences were used as inner fences in some areas. The *Grenztruppen* occasionally test-crashed vehicles into obstacles and walls to check their designs, with improvements made as a result.

Grenzwall 75

In 1976 construction of the fourth-generation wall commenced. By 1980 there were still third- and even second-generation walls in place. Grenzwall 75 was a state-of-the-art prefab barrier, essentially person- and vehicle-proof plus

comparatively quick and easy to install. It required less maintenance and was more durable. The modular wall section, officially known as a *Stützwandelement UL 12.11* (retaining wall element), was made of reinforced concrete and was L-shaped in cross-section. Each element was 3.6m high, 1.2m wide, and the platform base was 1.6m deep. At the base each element was 22cm thick and 12cm at the top. Each 2,750kg element was hoisted into place (using recessed lifting rings) and set on a thin, poured-concrete foundation to ensure it was level and to bond it to the ground. Precision was everything: the vertical ends needed to be closely aligned, and they featured tongue-and-grooves for a snug fit. The long, horizontal portion of the base of the L shape was positioned facing east. The top edge also had to be perfectly straight. The ends of a horizontal steel reinforcing bar protruded near the top end of each element, and these were welded together as each element was positioned. The seams and hoisting holes were then cemented or tarred. Sections of 30cm-diameter sewer pipe with 14cm-wide slots cut along their length were cemented in place on the top of each element. This grey or black bituminous pipe was 5cm thick. One element cost 359 Ostmarks and some 45,000 were emplaced, totalling 16,155,000 Ostmarks (for comparison, a loaf of bread cost 1.04 Ostmarks). For reasons of cost, they were only used for the outer wall. In total, 106km of the border was faced with *Stützwandelement UL 12.11.*

In some areas, 6m or wider harrowed control strips paralleled the outer wall, while in others most of the area enclosed by the outer wall and inner fence (comprising bare sandy soil) served as a control strip. To prevent vehicles attempting to crash through the Wall, V- and square-shaped ditches, steel hedgehogs and fields of spikes ('Stalin's grass') were emplaced.

Floodlights, set atop steel and concrete poles in kilometre-long lines (*Lichttrosse*), illuminated the cleared strip and the interior side of the Wall. PSG-80 sentinel signal devices (*Postensignalgerät*) – trip flares – also formed part of the system. The PSG-80 comprised a flare cartridge on a small wire tripod or stake, with 30–50cm-high tripwires running in both directions parallel to the Wall. When tripped, the magnesium flare burned for about a minute illuminating a 100m radius; some PSG-80s made a flash-bang report.

An electronic-sensor signal fence (as used on the IGB hinterland) was emplaced in the security zone. The alarm signals rang out in towers and command centres, and alarm lights (*Signalgerät*) were fitted atop 4m-high steel poles all along the fence. If the fence was disturbed, a red light flashed and a horn sounded to alert foot and motorized patrols. It was also hoped that this would persuade escapees to turn back. A green light flashed during testing procedures, which also signalled to escapees that the fence was active (it was sometimes turned off).

From the mid-1970s, BT-11 observation towers and *Führungsstelle* command towers began replacing the earlier wooden and steel examples. Some BT-9 towers were also emplaced. Two types of tower unique to Berlin appeared in the 1980s. One type was a control tower

A *Grenzer* looks on from behind a temporary fence as the new Grenzwall 75 is erected in the background. In the foreground is the memorial to Olga Segler, an East German killed when attempting to escape over the Wall. (IWM CT 1495)

Berlin Wall barriers and facilities, August 1989	
Outer walls and fencing	162km
Outer L-shaped element walls (included in the above total)	106km
Signal fencing	127.5km
Patrol roads	172km
Anti-vehicle ditches	124.3km
Hedgehog anti-vehicle obstacles	19km
Control strips	165km
Floodlight pole lines	166km
Hinterland outer fencing	68km
Guard towers	302
Observation bunkers	20
Dog runs	259

This illustration shows a section of retaining wall (*Stützwandelement UL 12.11*) from the Grenzwall 75 phase of the Berlin Wall. It is topped with a section of 30cm-diameter sewer pipe, to prevent anyone climbing it from getting a good grip. The two holes in the front face are for lifting the wall into place. This section measures 3.6m high and 1.2m wide, and the platform base is 1.6m deep. The base of the wall is 22cm thick, whereas at the top it is 12cm thick.

A view into the East Berlin side from the Bernauerstraße observation platform in the French sector. Lacking space for an anti-vehicle ditch, four rows of hedgehogs have been emplaced. In the centre can be seen a watchdog's shelter. The outer wall is of the Grenzwall 75 type. (IWM TR 30283-10)

West and East Berlin, 1989

1. Bomholmer Straße/Bösebrücke
   West Berlin and BRD citizens
2. Chausseestraße/Reinickendorfer Straße
   West Berlin citizens
3. Invalidenstraße/Sandkrungbrücke
   West Berlin citizens
4. Friedrichstraße
   Railroad station
5. Checkpoint Charlie/Friedrichstraße
   Foreigners and diplomats
6. Heinrich-Heinestraße/Prinzenstraße
   BRD citizens
7. Oberbaumbrücke
   West Berlin citizens

8. Sonnenallee
   West Berlin citizens
9. Walthersdorfer Chausee
   West Berlin citizens and foreigners to Schönefeld Airport
10. Checkpoint Bravo/Dreilinden/Drewitz
    Autobahn transit to BRD
11. Griebnitzsee/Wannsee
    Rail transit to BRD
12. Heerstraße
    Non-autobahn transit to BRD
13. Staaken/Spandau
    Rail transit to BRD
14. Stolpe/Heiligensee
    Autobahn transit to BRD

● Crossing points
◉ Crossing points existing in 1961
✈ Airport
— The Wall

for autobahn and railway entry points. It consisted of a 1m-square, 6m-high column, on top of which was perched a 1.8×1.8m observation compartment with three windows in each sides, a spotlight on top and a loudspeaker mounted on the side. An alternative low-cost, prefabricated tower featured six, stacked 1.8×1.8m-square, 1m-high light concrete sections, topped with a slightly wider sheet-metal observation compartment with three windows on each side.

The Grenzwall 75 security zone varied greatly between sections, depending on available ground and the risk and frequency of escapes in each particular area. Many buildings were torn down to widen the original border zone, which varied from 100m to 200m. Towers and lines of floodlight poles could be positioned anywhere within the security zone. From the interior fence or wall to the outer wall and the West, a typical security zone arrangement was as follows (note that the distance between each barrier varied with intervening strips of bare ground):

- Inner (hinterland) 3–4m-high steel mesh fence, or old-type wall with barbed wire.
- 3m-high signal fence.
- Dog run (not always present).
- Trip flares.
- Patrol road (asphalt).
- Control strip.
- Anti-vehicle ditch.
- Anti-vehicle obstacles (hedgehogs, tyre spikes).
- 3.2–4.2m-high outer frontier wall or fence.

The 43.1km wall dividing the city – the Intra-city Frontier (*Innerstädtische Grenze Berlin*) – is what most people think of as the Berlin Wall. However, there was also 111.9km of what was known as the 'country wall' or 'Ring around Berlin' (*Ring um Berlin*) circling the rest of West Berlin. While much of this portion was bordered by forests and fields, suburban areas and communities also abutted it. In the early days, many were able to escape through this less protected, under-guarded area. Its best protection was that it was more difficult to access and cross by foot. *Grenztruppen* and Vopo patrols were very active on the approaches and Border Helpers were recruited among locals. The Stasi were especially active throughout the Berlin area, attempting to discover escape plots. The country wall was gradually reinforced, but was still the weakest portion of the Ring. There were several rivers, canals and lakes in and around Berlin. These were patrolled by both *Grenztruppen* and *Wasserschutzpolizei* boats.[3] DDR maps of East Berlin showed only a few main boulevards in West Berlin – the rest was blank. The same applied to maps of the DDR: the BRD side was blank, as was the 5km restricted frontier zone.

Military police representatives of the Western Allies – from left to right, French, British and American – in front of the Kommandatura in West Berlin. (IWM MH 030871)

3 BRD Water Protection Police boats had vivid cornflower-blue hulls with white decks and superstructures, and hull numbers preceded by 'WSP'. DDR WSP boats were all light grey with hull numbers preceded by 'WS'.

From West Germany to West Berlin

Regardless of the existence of the Wall, West Berlin was accessible from the BRD by land, air and water. Four autobahns crossed into the DDR, with the southern two merging into one. The main southern autobahn crossed the frontier at Rudolfstein-Hirschberg near Hof (BRD) close to the Czechoslovak border and entering southern West Berlin. Another autobahn ran east from Herleshausen-Wartha to link up with the southern route near Gera (DDR). The central route crossed at Helmstedt-Marienorn to southern Berlin. The northern route crossed at Gudow Zarrentin and connected to Berlin on its north-west side. There were also three main rail routes. In the south three lines crossed the DDR frontier (east to west) at Bebra-Gerstungen, Ludwigsstadt and Hof-Guternfurst, the main line with which the other two merged. The central rail line crossed the frontier near Wolfsburg and ran due east to Berlin. The northern line ran from Schwanheide-Büchen south-east to Berlin. The three air routes originated from several departure airports in northern, central and southern BRD, but merged into three separate air corridors to West Berlin's Tegel, Gatow and Tempelhof airports. The main barge route ran from the inland port of Hanover (BRD) east to Berlin. A northern route originated at the seaport of Hanover. Inside the DDR it split and both canals connected with the Hanover-Berlin Canal.

The autobahn, rail and canal crossing points were heavily guarded with kilometre-long walls running parallel to them prior to entering the city. This prevented escapees from boarding vehicles, boats and trains. There were remotely controlled gates that could slide shut or rise up rapidly, and vehicles, trains and water craft were detail searched (sometimes with dogs). Travel on the autobahn required transit visas (*Trovárishch*) with vehicle description, names and addresses of passengers, purpose of the trip, goods being transported, amount of money, and date of return. Departure and expected arrival times were specified. Westerners could not deviate from the authorized route, nor could they take photographs. If they arrived late they could be accused of deviating or making unauthorized stops. There were instances when Westerners were arrested and jailed without notifying the Western authorities; some were even found in prisons after the Wall fell. Conversely, if Westerners arrived early then they might be accused of exceeding the 60km/h speed limit – a marked contrast with West Germany's unlimited-speed autobahns. The control and security measures would be increased during times of East–West tension as a feeble but irritating means of harassment.

A verbal confrontation between a BRD Water Protection Police boat (right) and its DDR counterpart (left) on a Berlin waterway.

When the Wall fell in 1989, plans were being prepared for a modern, high-tech wall. It involved the continuation of upgrading older barriers to Grenzwall 75 standards, but more electronic sensors, motion detectors, acoustic sensors, and remote low-light level television surveillance cameras would be employed to reduce manpower levels.

MANNING THE WALL AND THE IGB

To secure, patrol and support the many kilometres of border completely surrounding East Germany and West Berlin required a considerable number of specialized troops and equipment. The *Grenztruppen*, usually called 'Border Troops' in the West, fielded a strength of up to 50,000 personnel, the equivalent of three divisions.

From May 1945 Soviet Border Troops (*Pogranichnyie Voiska*) of the NKVD (KGB from 1954) secured the border and manned crossing points. The *Deutsche Grenzpolizei* (DGP, German Frontier Police) was organized under the *Innenministeriums zum Schutz der Staatsgrenze* (Interior Ministry for Security of the State Frontier) on 1 December 1946. This paramilitary force was a full-time organization quartered in barracks, with units assigned specific sectors. Soviet troops still manned crossing points alongside the DGP. They were initially under the control of the five state police chiefs. In November 1948 they were subordinated to the *Hauptabteilung Grenzpolizei/Bereitschaften* (Main Section Frontier Police/Alert Unit) of the *Deutsche Verwaltung des Innern* (DVdI, German Administration of the Interior). The *Grenzpolizei* were placed under the *Hauptabteilung Grenzpolizei* in July 1949, but still under the DVdI. In October after a ministerial reorganization it was made subordinate to the *Hauptverwaltung Deutsche Volkspolizei der Ministerium des Innern* (MdI, Main Administration of the Ministry of Interior). In 1952 they separated from the Vopos under their own *Hauptverwaltung Deutsche Grenzpolizei*, but still under the MdI. It was almost immediately turned over to the *Ministerium für Staatssicherheit* (MfS). Being a political football it was again transferred to the MdI in 1953, in 1955 it returned to the control of the MfS, and then back to the MdI in 1957. In 1954/55 the DGP assumed control of the frontier and crossing points from the Soviets. The only Soviet troops still involved with the border were in East Berlin and at the Helmstedt-Marienorn Autobahn crossing point. Heavy weapons were assigned for the first time, followed by tanks and self-propelled artillery in 1959, and infantry training was introduced.

With the building of the Wall and the complete closure of the border in 1961, it was decided that the protection of the frontier was a military matter. The border system would be integrated into the defence of the state. The GDP was transferred to the *Ministerium für Nationale Verteidigung* (MfNV, Ministry of National Defence), expanded and reorganized into a military force. The new organization was the *Grenztruppen der Nationale Volksarmee*, effective 15 September 1961. This was a separate branch of service of the NVA, the *Grenzkommando* (Frontier Command), and was responsible for frontier security and defence on the

A *Grenztruppen Soldat* (soldier) and *Gefreiter* (corporal) in the old service uniform, reminiscent of World War II. In the background is a BT-11 observation tower and a Trabant patrol car.

West German, Czechoslovak and Polish borders, the Baltic Sea coast and the Berlin Wall. Under the NVA the *Grenztruppen* were reorganized with fewer heavy weapons, and in 1963 regiments were reduced in strength owing to manpower shortages.

As a result of international diplomatic forcereduction discussions in 1973, the *Grenztruppen* were transferred to the MdI on 28 February 1974 so that they would not be liable to any force-reduction agreements. While the regular armed forces might be reduced, the DDR would not dare down-size the *Grenztruppen* and risk its citizens voting with their feet. Their title was changed to *Grenztruppen der DDR.*

Service in the *Grenztruppen* was equivalent to duty in the NVA. The rank-and-file were conscripted soldiers serving 18 months and liable for service from age 18 to 26. Volunteers could sign up for three years and often obtained junior NCO rank. Career NCOs served for at least 10 years and warrant officers for at least 15. Reserve officers only had to serve three years on active duty, but career officers served at least 25. The *Grenztruppen* had a higher percentage of professional troops than most other services; only 50 per cent were conscripts.

Grenztruppen newspaper recruiting ads for three-year, long-service volunteers promised higher technical education opportunities for civilian employment after discharge, job placement assistance, frequent promotions, living quarters at their duty station, and career development. Requirements specified at least a polytechnic high-school 10th-grade education, completion of technical labourer apprenticeship, pre-military training with the Sport and Technical Society (*Gesellschaft für Sport und Technik,* GST) in school, Class C driving licence, and good health.

A rather sloppy looking *Grenztruppen Unterleutnant* (junior lieutenant) in a service uniform at an encampment outside of East Berlin, preparing for a parade. The NVA tended to display an appearance less than worthy of German military traditions, including longish hair.

Grenztruppen met the same criteria as other NVA soldiers, except for special requirements regarding their place of residence and political reliability. Those with a record of dissent, including immediate family members, or who were actively religious, were sent to other branches of the NVA. The main criteria was that they could not reside in areas near the IGB, nor have immediate relatives in the BRD. Troops were assigned to frontier sectors distant from their homes. Those from Berlin's environs were assigned to the IGB. The government did not want former *Grenztruppen* using their knowledge to aid escapees.

Conscription occurred in May and November. Recruits underwent training and indoctrination in a training regiment. They learned basic military skills (like other Warsaw Pact soldiers) in only four weeks: physical fitness, close-order drill, weapons, firing practice, individual battle drills; chemical, atomic and biological protection; and map reading, first aid and hygiene. In the barracks they were taught disciplinary regulations, duties and rights of soldiers, complaint procedures, on- and off-duty behaviour, garrison and guard duty responsibilities, and their rights regarding pay, leave and rations. Over the next five months they received speciality training. This included most of the skills necessary to man towers and frontier crossing stations, inspect vehicles, conduct identity checks, recognize falsified documents, search suspects, take photographs, emplace

The *Grenzpolizei* were originally armed with German World War II weapons including 9mm P.38 pistols, 9mm MP.40 machine pistols, 7.9mm Kar.98k bolt-action carbines, 7.9mm Stg.44 assault rifles, and 7.9mm MG.34 and MG.42 machine guns. They soon received Soviet World War II and immediate post-war weapons: TT-33 pistols, PPSh-41 submachine guns, SKS semi-automatic carbines, M1944 bolt-action carbines, DPM and RP-46 light machine guns, SG-43 and SGM heavy machine guns, and 40mm RPG-2 anti-tank projectors. All small arms were 7.62mm, but using three different cartridges. The PPSh-41, what the NVA called the MPi41 machine pistol, virtually became a symbol of the *Grenzpolizei*.

Beginning in 1960, they began to receive modern weapons, as did the rest of the NVA. East Germany by now was producing its own versions of Soviet weapons (the Soviet designations are given in parentheses). The DDR versions were typically of better quality than the Soviet originals: 9mm Pistole M (PM), MPiK and MPiKM (AK-47 and AKM) assault rifles, IMGK and IMGD (RPK and RPD) light machine guns, RP46 (RP-46) and sMGK (PK) machine guns, 12.7mm sMG38 (DShKM38/46) anti-aircraft machine guns, and 40mm RPG-7 anti-tank projectors. Unless otherwise stated, all were 7.62mm using two different cartridges. They later received the 5.45mm MPiK74N (AK-74S) assault rifle and RPG-18 single-shot, disposal anti-tank rocket launcher. (The USSR did not permit the DDR to produce heavy weapons, armoured fighting vehicles, missiles, or combat aircraft.)

The *Grenztruppen* were also provided with older heavy equipment, including T-34/85 tanks, 76mm SU-76M and 85mm SU-85 assault guns, BTR-152V wheeled armoured personnel carriers, 57mm ZiS-2 and 85mm D-44 anti-tank guns, 82mm B-10 and 107mm B-11 recoilless guns (later 73mm SPG-9 recoilless guns), and 82mm PM-37 and 120mm HM-43 mortars.

mines, inspect border barriers, and conduct patrols. Their marksmanship training went beyond that of the regular NVA. They had to hit two moving targets at 200m with just four shots, day or night. Some 50 per cent of their training time was ideological indoctrination, being taught they were the first line of defence against Western imperialism, spies and provocateurs. Their official mission was the prevention of border breakthroughs as well as effective protection from acts of terror. No leave or passes were granted during training.

There were also schools and training units for officer candidates, warrant officers and NCOs. The *Grenztruppen* had their own signals, maintenance, transport, supply, medical, administrative and other speciality personnel. There was special training available for dog handling, technical security and surveillance equipment, radio monitoring, boat handling and reconnaissance missions. Once assigned to a unit, training continued with additional speciality training, cross-training in related skills, and unit tactical training. Guards were awarded special qualification badges in one of three grades, and higher grades could be awarded after annual testing.

Once assigned to a unit the reality of their duty to the state became apparent. They were to shoot, without orders, any person attempting to cross to the West. It was made clear that any failure on their part to defend the frontier or attempt to escape would result in repercussions on them and their families. Maintaining good morale was a constant problem during the 18 months of long, lonely, sometimes dull and sometimes highly stressful service as a *Grenzer*.

Grenztruppen units

From the beginning, the *Grenzpolizei* and *Grenztruppen* steadily increased in size. By 1959 the *Grenzpolizei* were organized into sections: Interzonal Border (*Innerzonal Grenz*), International Border (*International Grenz*), North (*Nord*) and Berlin Ring (*Berliner Ring*) sections (*Abteilungen*). Assigned to the sections were 22 regimental-size frontier alert units (*Grenzbereitschaften*) with

Frontier Troops Command	Grenztruppen Kommando (Pätz)
English	German
Command Staff, Frontier Troops Command	*Führungsstab, Grenztruppen Kommando (Pätz)*
Officer Higher School for Frontier Troops	*Offiziershochschule der Grenztruppen 'Rosa Luxemburg' (Suhl)*
Music Corps	*Musikkorps (Suhl)*
Warrant Officer and Frontier Indoctrination School	*Fähnrich- und Grenzaufklärerschule (Suhl)*
Warrant Officer School	*Fähnrichschule (Nordhausen)*
NCO School VI	*Unteroffiziersschule VI 'Egon Schultz' (Perleberg)*
NCO School for Technical Signals	*Unteroffiziersschule für Nachrichtentechnik (Frandkfurt)*
Helicopter Unit 16	*Hubschrauberstaffel 16 'Albert Kuntz' (Salzwedel)*
Guard and Security Post Battalion 16	*Wach- und Sicherstellungsbataillon 16 (Pätz)*
Radio Service 16	*Funkdienst 16 (Pätz)*
Signals Repair Company 16	*Nachrichteninstandsetzungskompanie 16 (Motzen)*
Signals Transmitter Central	*Funksendezentrale Märkisch-Buchholz*
Guard Company	*Wachkompanie (Motzen)*
Staff Music Corps	*Stabsmuskikkorps (Erfurt)*
Service Dog School	*Diensthundeschule (Postdam-Sago)*
Maintenance Company 16	*Wartungskompanie 16 (Motzen und Pätz)*
Motor Transport Company 16	*Kraftfahrzeug-Kompanie 16 (Pätz)*
Public Relations Company 16	*Propagandakompanie 16 (Schenkendorf)*

Frontier Troops Command North	Grenztruppen Kommando Nord (Stendal)
English	German
Staff Company 25	Stabskompanie 25 (Stendal)
Frontier Regiment 6	Grenzregiment 6 'Hans Kollwitz' (Schönberg)
Frontier Regiment 8	Grenzregiment 8 'Robert Abshgen' (Grabow)
Frontier Regiment 20	Grenzregiment 20 'Martin Schwants' (Haldberstadt)
Frontier Regiment 23	Grenzregiment 23 'Wilhelm Bahnik' (Klabe/Milde)
Frontier Regiment 24	Grenzregiment 24 'Fritz Heckert' (Salzwedel)
Frontier Training Regiment 5	Grenzausbildungsregiment 5 'Gustav Sobottke' (Glöwen/T. Potsdam)
Frontier Training Regiment 7	Grenzausbildungsregiment 7 'Martin Hoop' (Haldstadte)
Security Company 25	Sicherungskompanie 25 (Dingelstedt)
Motor Transport Company 25	Kraftfahrzeug-Kompanie 25 (Stendal)
Construction Company 25	Baukompamie 25 (Gardelegen/Oschersleben)
Pioneer Company 25	Pionierkompanie 25 (Gardelegen)

Frontier Troops Command South	Grenztruppen Kommando Sud (Erfurt)
Staff Company 27	Stabskompanie 27 (Erfurt)
Frontier Regiment 1	Grenzregiment 1 'Eugen Levine' (Mühlhausen)
Frontier Regiment 3	Grenzregiment 3 'Florian Geyer' (Dermbach)
Frontier Regiment 4	Grenzregiment 4 'Willi Gebhardt' (Heiligenstadt)
Frontier Regiment 9	Grenzregiment 9 'Comrad Blenkle' (Meiningen)
Frontier Regiment 10	Grenzregiment 10 'Ernst Grube' (Plauen)
Frontier Regiment 15	Grenzregiment 15 'Herbert Warnke' (Eisenach)
Frontier Training Regiment 11	Grenzausbildungsregiment 11 'Theodor Neubauer' (Eisenach)
Frontier Training Regiment 12	Grenzausbildungsregiment 12 'Rudi Arnstadt' (Plauen)
Staff and Provisions Battalion 27	Stabs- und Versorgungsbataillon 27 (Erfurt)
Security Company 27	Sicherungskompanie 27 (Neustädt)
Construction Company 27	Baukompamie 27 (Eisenach)
Pioneer Company 27	Pionierkompanie 27 (Hildburghausen)

Frontier Troops Command Centre	Grenztruppen Kommando Mitte (Berlin-Karlshorst)
Staff Company 26	Stabskompanie 26 (Berlin-Karlshorst)
Frontier Regiment 33	Grenzregiment 33 'Heinrich Dorrenbach' (Berlin-Treptow)
Frontier Regiment 34	Grenzregiment 34 'Hanno Günther' (Groß Glienicke)
Frontier Regiment 35	Grenzregiment 35 'Nikolai Bersarin' (Berlin-Niederschönhausen)
Frontier Regiment 36	Grenzregiment 36 'Helmut Poppe' (Berlin-Rummelsburg)
Frontier Regiment 38	Grenzregiment 38 'Clara Zetkin' (Hennigsdorf)
Frontier Regiment 42	Grenzregiment 42 'Fritz Perlitz' (Kleinmachnow)
Frontier Regiment 44	Grenzregiment 44 'Walter Junker' (Potsdam-Babelsberg)
Frontier Crossing Point Security Regiment 26	Grenzübergangsstellensicherungsregiment 26 'Walter Husemann' (Berlin-Niederschönhausen)
Frontier Training Regiment 39	Grenzausbildungregiment 39 'Ho Chi Minh' (Berlin-Wilhelmshagen)
Frontier Training Regiment 40	Grenzausbildungregiment 40 'Hans Coppi' (Oranienburg)
Artillery Regiment 26	Artillerieregiment 26 (Belin-Johannesthal)
Missile Projector Battalion 26	Geschoßwerferabteilung 26 (Schildow)
Security Company 26	Sicherungskompanie 26 (Waltersdorf)
Chemical Defence Company 26	Chemische-Abwehr-Kompanie 26 (Groß Glienicke)
Construction Company 26	Baukompanie 26 (Berlin-Treptow)
Motor Transport Company 26	Kraftfahrzeug-Kompanie 26 (Groß Glienicke)
Pioneer Company 26	Pionierkompanie 26 (Groß Glienicke)
Training Establishment for Service Dogs	Ausbildungseinrichtung für Diensthunde (Berlin-Niederschönhausen)

Grenztruppen mobility

The Grenztruppen used both Soviet and domestic-built trucks and cars. Among these were the Ural 375D, KraZ 214 and Tatra 148 trucks. The most infamous was the little Trabant 601 Kübel, also known as the Tabbi, Rennpappe ('running pasteboard'), Plastikbomber (owing to its plastic body). It could carry four men, and these small, open-sided cars were used for fence patrols and delivering relief guards. Trabants, which today are considered nostalgic relics of the DDR, were heavy polluters and notoriously underpowered with a two-stroke, two-cylinder engine. When making their way up even a gently sloping patrol road, passengers would have to dismount and walk beside them. Motorradwerk Zschopau (MZ) ETZ250 and TS250/1/A motorcycles were also used.

A small number of Soviet-built helicopters were employed by the Grenzflieger for frontier surveillance and to deliver reaction forces. These included Mi-2 Hoplite, Mi-8 Hip and Mi-24 Hind helicopters. The camouflage-painted helicopters bore the round DDR aircraft national emblem on a bright-green diamond backing.

The 6. Grenzbrigade Küste operated almost 550 watercraft. These varied over time, but in 1989 the large craft consisted of 18 Kondor I patrol boats and 13 seagoing guard boats (Wachboote Bremse-Klasse), plus large numbers of small harbour and canal patrol boats mostly manned by three-man crews, as were the Border Command Centre's river patrol boats.

Grenztruppen vehicles could be forest green, olive drab or camouflage painted. The circular black, red and gold-backed DDR coat of arms had a bright-green border. Black-on-white vehicle identification plates were marked 'GT' with a four-digit number. Grenztruppen patrol boats were medium grey with 'G' preceding the hull number.

6th Frontier Coast Brigade English	6. Grenzbrigade Küste (Rostock) Deutsch
Staff Company 6	Stabskompanie 6 (Rostock)
Frontier Battalion 2	Grenzrbataillon 2 (Stubbenkammer)
Frontier Battalion 3	Grenzrbataillon 3 (Graal Müritz)
Frontier Battalion 4	Grenzrbataillon 4 (Tarnewitz)
Frontier Training Battalion 5	Grenzrausbildungbataillon 5 (Kühlungsborn)
1st Frontier Ship Detachment	1. Grenzschiffsabteilung (Warnemünde)
2nd Frontier Ship Detachment	2. Grenzschiffsabteilung (Warnemünde)
3rd Frontier Ship Detachment	3. Grenzschiffsabteilung (Warnemünde)
2nd, 3rd, 6th, 7th & 8th Frontier Boat Groups	2., 3., 6., 7. und 8.Grenzbootgruppen
four Water [patrol] Companies	vier Wasser Kompanien
Frontier Company 1	Grenzkompanie 1 Bansin
Frontier Signals Company 6	Grenznachrichtenkompanie 6 (Rostock)
Frontier Security Company 6	Grenzsicherungskompanie 6 (Rostock)
8th Frontier Technical Observation Company	8. Technische Beobachtungskompanie (Warnemünde)
NCO Training Company 6	Unteroffiziersausbildungskompanie 6 (Rostock)
four Frontier Crossing Stations Water	vier Grenzübergangsstellen Wasser

seven different schools and four supply depots. Alert units (regiments) received heavy weapons battalions in 1956 and an alert (reaction force) company. The regiments were organized into six brigades. Brigade tank companies and artillery batteries were assigned in 1960.

In 1962 many of the heavy weapons were withdrawn and BTR-152V armoured personnel carriers were restricted to headquarters' use. Owing to manpower shortages, the regiments lost their alert companies and a battalion headquarters, and the brigades lost their tank companies. The sealing of the IGB and of West Berlin meant that all available troops were needed as guards, and not for manning unneeded heavy weapons.

A *Grenztruppen Motorradwerk Zschopau (MZ) ETZ250* motorcycle.

In February 1971 the Frontier Command at Pätz was reorganized to control units in specific areas. Frontier Command North (*Grenzekommando Nord*) headquartered at Stendal secured the IGB from the Baltic Sea to Goslar (FGR) – about half the IGB's length. Frontier Command South (*Grenzkommando Sud 'Hermann Jahn'*) at Erfut controlled the southern portion from Goslar to the Czechoslovak border at Rehu (BRD). Border Command Central (*Grenzkommando Mitte*) was at Berlin-Karlshorst and responsible for the ring around West Berlin. There were three smaller commands, the largest being 6th Frontier Brigade Coast (*6. Grenzbrigade Küste*) at Rostock near the Baltic Sea, sometimes incorrectly known as 'Frontier Command Coast'. The Coast Brigade was under the operational control of the *Kriegsmarine* (German Navy) while the *Grenzkommando* had administrative control and support. Brigade personnel wore navy-style uniforms. Two frontier sectors manned by only a few hundred troops operated crossing stations on the western and southern borders: *Grenzabschnitt Volks Republik Polen 'Hermann Gartmann'* at Frankfurt (Oder) and *Grenzabschnitt Tschechoslowakei 'Walter Breidfeld'* at

Pirna. These units were reportedly designated Frontier Regiments 18 and 19 in the 1970s/1980s. Both sectors were organized into six frontier subsectors (*Grenzunterabschnitt I–VI*) overseeing 52 frontier sector posts (*Grenzabschnittsposten*). Most frontier regiments and some other units were bestowed honorific titles bearing the names of socialist heroes.

Frontier regiments on the IGB were organized into a staff company (*Stabkompanie*), signals company (*Nachrichtenkompanie*), pioneer company (*Pionierekompanie*), and three frontier battalions (*I–III Grenzbataillonen*). The battalions had a staff company and typically four frontier companies (*Grenzkompanien*). Occasionally one battalion per regiment might have had three, five or six companies. Regardless of the number of companies, they were numbered in sequence through the regiment. In the case of normal 400–450-man four-company battalions these were: I GBtl (1–4), II GBtl (5–8), III GBtl (9–12). The 100–120-man companies were organized into three, three-group (*Grupp* – equivalent to a squad) platoons (*Zug*) plus a *Grenzaufklärungszug* (Gak, Frontier Reconnaissance Platoon). Regimental companies bore the parent regiment's number, e.g. *Stabkompanie 4* of GRgt 4. Regiments were responsible for operating varied numbers of highway (*Autobahn*), road (*Straße*), railway (*Eisenbahn*) and water (*Wasser*) frontier crossing stations (*Grenübergangsstelle*, GÜSt). Each *Grenzkompanie* had its own *Kaserne* (barracks) located in its sector.

The seven frontier regiments around Berlin were organized differently, with much variance in their internal structure depending on their missions. Typically they consisted of five frontier companies (1–5), a staff company, an artillery and mortar battery (*Artillerie- und Granatwerferbatterie* – two different batteries in some regiments), and motor transport, signals and pioneer companies, plus varied numbers of frontier crossing stations. Some possessed a boat company (*Bootkompanie*) for patrolling canals and rivers.

The DDR was awash with internal security organizations to protect it from capitalist corruption. All were involved to varying degrees with border security and coordinated with the *Grenztruppen* though the MfS. While they did not secure the border itself, they tracked and inspected vehicle traffic, reported suspicious and disloyal persons, and helped conduct searches in areas adjacent to the frontier. The Vopos (under the MdI) handled civil police duties and included the Protection (*Schutzpolizei* – regular police), Traffic (*Verkehrspolizei* – highway patrol) and Criminal (*Kriminalpolizei* – investigators) Police. There were three paramilitary organizations under the Vopo. The Security Alert Police (*Bereitschaftpolizei* – Bepo) was organized into 21 mobile battalions for riot control and securing government facilities. The Transport Police (*Transportpolizei* – Trapo) with eight companies were mainly responsible for railway and yard security. The Water Protection Police (*Wasserschutzpolizei* – WSP) operated river patrol boats on inland waterways, regulating boat and barge traffic and ensuring safety compliance. The Battle Groups of the Working Class (*Kamphfgruppen der Arbeitklasse* – KG),

The infamous Trabant 601 Kübel, the underpowered and heavily polluting patrol car of the *Grenztruppen*. It is painted a dull olive green with the black, red and gold DDR coat of arms encircled in bright green, the latter identifying it as a *Grenztruppen* vehicle.

often called the 'Workers' Militia' in the West, was a voluntary, paramilitary, part-time, rear-area security force. It was organized into some 200 battalions stationed throughout the country. Its manpower could be mobilized for search and cordon operations.

There were also Ministry for State Security (Stasi) personnel assigned to the *Grenztruppen* down to company level. Stasi personnel were indistinguishable from *Grenztruppen*, wearing the same uniforms and insignia. They were assigned to the 6th Section in command, regiment, and battalion headquarters. They included a counterintelligence element, recruiting informers within units. It was estimated that one in ten officers and one in 30 enlisted men were informers. The Stasi maintained a file on every unit member. All personnel were routinely interviewed, and this was when informers passed on their information. There were also means through which to pass on information of immediate importance. The Stasi intelligence element collected information on NATO activities, and strove to recruit sympathizers among BRD military, police and civilians – though they were not always successful in this. The Stasi also supervised the companies' frontier reconnaissance platoon, and the passport-control section at crossing stations were entirely manned by Stasi.

The *Grenztruppen* also employed over 3,000 Volunteer Helpers of the Frontier Troops (*Freiwillige Helfer der Grenztruppen*), a programme formally implemented in 1953. These were auxiliary personnel at least 18 years old volunteering to assist the regular guards by relieving them on weekends. They would man guard towers crossing stations, and conduct foot patrols. They were selected for their political reliability and underwent exhaustive Stasi background checks. They were usually unarmed, but could carry weapons if approved by the battalion commander. They would also assist when there were nearby public events on either side of the border, and were especially active in the summer months on the coast when tourists flocked to the beaches. They also did undercover work in civilian clothes, reported rumours and malcontents within the frontier population, and kept an eye on strangers near the border. They wore standard uniforms, but, other than a green armband, were without insignia. Civilians, including teenagers, living within and adjacent to the frontier zone were encouraged to report suspicious persons and spy on neighbours.

The *Grenztruppen* leadership was involved through meetings and conferences with local mayors, the Vopo and other state agencies and security organs to foster cooperation. They shared information with the aim of reducing crime. They participated in local activities such as festivals and celebrations. *Grenztruppen* rank-and-file sometimes took part in local civic action projects such as harvest time, and road clean up and repairs.

Frontier guard duty

Life in the *Grenztruppen*, as in any Warsaw Pact army, was monotonous, harsh and Spartan. It was even harder in the *Grenztruppen* owing to the long duty hours and loneliness of their shifts in remote areas, constant surveillance and monitoring, segregation from the local population, poor pay and the stress of their assignment. Barracks life was severe with poor rations, limited heating, no hot water, and harassment by longer-serving soldiers. While the pay was poor by Western standards, *Grenztruppen* did receive a small bonus for *Grenzdeinst* (frontier service) and annual bonuses were distributed to exemplary individuals.

Restrictions prevented watching or listening to Western television or radio, and the possession of Western newspapers and magazines. Guards would sometimes covertly trade NVA manuals and insignia with NATO soldiers or West Germany Zolls for men's magazines and liquor, even though any contact with Westerners was forbidden. They would also hide West German newspapers that had blown over the border, even though finding such material on them meant interrogation, barracks arrest and even court-martial. Telephone calls and mail were monitored, and there were informers within units.

Enlisted men received 18 days' annual leave, with NCOs and officers receiving more. Only 15 per cent of a unit were allowed leave at any one time. Upon return from leave, soldiers were interviewed by their commander about what they did and who they saw. This was to assess their morale and continued reliability. If the soldier had personal or family problems, he might be given duty at restricted-zone control points rather than on the frontier. On the rare occasions when passes were issued, they were required to be in uniform, could travel only a limited distance, and had to return by 10 a.m.

Three eight-hour guard shifts were mounted daily at 4 a.m., 12 p.m. and 8 p.m. The actual duty day for the 4 a.m.–12 p.m. shift was from 2.30 a.m. –5.30 p.m. They then took the 12 p.m–8 p.m. shift with a duty day beginning at 8 a.m. and running until 10 p.m. Their next duty day for the 8 p.m.–4 a.m. shift began at 7 a.m. and finished at 7 p.m. Then they repeated the cycle. During the hours they were not on guard duty they had meals, cleaned barracks and equipment, drew and turned in weapons, stood guard mount to receive special instructions (*Vergatterung*), travelled to and from their guard posts, undertook classes and indoctrination, and were on stand by as a reaction force. With such disruptive sleep patterns, it was wearing duty.

Besides guards on the fence itself, personnel were needed to patrol the inner border fence, observe the hinterland, patrol throughout the restricted zone, man crossing stations, and guard the unit's own facilities. The mission of the *Grenztruppen* was to:

- Deter, detect and arrest violators of restricted zones.
- Prevent citizens, work details and guards from escaping to the West.
- Collect intelligence information on BRD and NATO forces and border activities.
- Collect domestic intelligence information on citizens in the frontier zone.
- Check the condition and maintenance of barriers, surveillance and alarm equipment, and related facilities.

The *Landgranze* (IGB) was divided into 58 frontier sectors (*Grenzabschitt*) typically of 20-plus kilometres in width, but they might be as little as 11km and as much as 32.5km. This depended on the terrain, vegetation and open areas, proximity of towns, and the road network. A frontier battalion might be assigned a 65–80km sector and a company 17–20km. Two of a regiment's battalions were responsible for the frontier itself, the third patrolled the hinterland, and the battalions rotated. Companies and platoons likewise would be reassigned from one sector to another. The standard procedure was for a company to assign all three platoons a sector. The platoon would man towers and observation posts, and conduct patrols. Later only one platoon per shift would man the entire company sector. It must be pointed out that the entire border was not under physical surveillance at all times. During daylight, manning was very light, but was heavier at night when most escape attempts were made. Fewer attempts were made in the winter, when snow showed tracks across the restricted zone before even reaching the barriers and vegetation was denuded of concealing leaves.

An observation bunker (*Erdbunker*) on the IGB

Front view

Rear view

G   AN OBSERVATION BUNKER (*ERDBUNKER*) ON THE IGB

The *Erdbunker* consists of three 0.8m-high, 1.6m-wide, 1.6m-deep sections of hollow concrete, stacked on top of each other; the seams were filled with cement. The bottom section is partly buried in the ground. The topmost section contains stepped firing ports. They were usually camouflaged. These bunkers appeared on the Intra-German Border. Access was via a door at the rear of the bunker.

Patrols, tower and observation-post teams comprised two men: the sentry leader (*Postenführer*) and the sentry (*Posten*). Often three-man patrols were employed at night. Guards were not assigned duty randomly. Friends and roommates were not assigned to the same patrols and the pairing of men did not become habitual. They were always switched and they did not know who they would be paired with until reporting for guard duty. However, friends would occasionally find themselves together because of men being given leave, undertaking training and work details, and other duties. Two-man patrols and tower teams were never to separate or be out of view of one another. Allowing this to happen – even when relieving oneself – resulted in disciplinary action. Company, platoon and group leaders inspecting guards travelled with another soldier. When relieving guards in a tower, one of the soldiers manning the tower descended and then the relieving soldier climbed into the tower. The next man to be relieved then descended and the last relieving man climbed up. This way there were always two men on the ground. A sergeant or officer of the guard who delivered the relief was also present. The orders were simple: if a guard attempted to defect, the other was to shoot him without warning.

The *Grenztruppen* medal for 'outstanding service'. The ribbons are dull red with a yellow central stripe and green edge stripes.

Whether on a patrol, in a guard tower or observation post, or at a crossing station, each assignment was designated a guard post (*Wachpost*). Foot patrols were the most visible of the activities. A patrol carried their assault rifles, basic

A *Grenztruppen Leutnant* (lieutenant) armed with an MPiKM assault rifle. He wears the standard NVA camouflage field uniform adopted in 1965. Called the 'rain drop' pattern in the West, the Germans called it the 'dashed print' (*Stricheldruck*).

load of ammunition, and an R-105 radio or KFG-78 field telephone. The telephone could be connected to terminals at checkpoints along the patrol road. The radios in a platoon were set on the same frequency, allowing them to talk to other patrols, towers and the platoon leader, who could talk to the company leader. They also carried DF or EDF 7×40 or Jena 6×30 binoculars, a 35mm Praktica camera and a reconnaissance journal. Some use was made of infrared night vision devices. The guards would photograph everything and everyone seen on the west side of the border and record all sightings in their journal. The thousands of photographs were forwarded weekly through channels to the MdI, and then were filed by date and frontier sector. Guards recorded the time and location of sightings, activity, description of persons (uniforms, equipment, organization), types of military/police vehicles and their bumper numbers, make and colour of civilian vehicles and their registration numbers, NATO patrol formations, new construction and so on. Using binoculars, they would determine the unit insignia, rank and names (from uniform name tags) of enemy personnel seen at the border. They referred to all NATO military and police personnel as the 'enemy'. Much of this was intended as low-level intimidation and to demonstrate they were ever-vigilant, photographing and recording everything. They often appeared to be taking photographs continuously, but in fact only took a few. The guards turned their backs if NATO personnel began photographing them. Vehicle patrols were less frequent than foot ones. These were conducted in Trabants, light trucks, motorcycles, and occasionally on bicycles. Snow skis were used in the winter and troops were issued white oversuits.

On patrol, the two men unhurriedly walked the road side by side. If unauthorized personnel were thought to be in the area, they would separate slightly, with one covering the other. They would be on the lookout for escapees, dropped personal items, footprints in the control strip, holes or attempted holes dug under the fence, cut fences or wires, mud on fence posts or mesh, clothing fragments on barbed wire, cut or damaged gate locks, and ladders, planks or tree branches leaning against the fence. They also looked for enemy activity on the west side of the fence, checked the electronic fences and trip flares, and watched for any natural damage or deterioration to barriers and border markers. Patrols would check in by radio or telephone at specific times or when reaching checkpoints. If they were not heard from, the sergeant of the guard was dispatched with a reaction force to check on the patrol. They were to be at the relief site at a specified time. Efforts were made not to establish a patrol pattern, varying them with each shift. A patrol could appear in any area from either direction at any time.

If tracks were detected in the control strip, or other signs of escape were discovered, the patrol marked the site with a small flag, notified superiors, and remained at the scene to protect it. The patrol leader entered the control strip and approached the tracks perpendicular to the line of movement and emplaced the marker near the tracks and inspected them without disturbing them. The *Posten* stepped off to the east side of the patrol road covering the *Postenführer* as he was near the fence. It is interesting that instructions and diagrams in manuals always depicted the border penetration and movement line to be from west to east rather than the (usual) opposite direction. A team would arrive to examine the site and determine how the escape was conducted, take photographs and make sketches. They were always on the lookout for any new and novel escape means. After a report had been made, the footprints were raked out and any evidence and escape materials were removed. If there was damage to the barriers or mines had detonated, pioneers made repairs.

Sometimes patrols were positioned in hidden sites on the edge of tree lines or camouflaged bunkers from which they could observe the 500m zone, the fence, and activity in the West. They remained hidden photographing (with telephoto lenses), recording, and reporting information. If occupying a known bunker, efforts were made to make it appear unoccupied with no outside activity. In temporary observation posts, standard field camouflage measures were used.

Guards used a password and challenge system to identify patrols or detect violators they might encounter at night. A guard would shout, '*Halt! Grenzposten. Parole!*' ('Halt! Frontier sentry. Password!') The person challenged would give the password, often the name of a city or town. The guard would then respond with the challenge, another noun beginning with the same letter, and '*Sie können passieren.*'

Guarding work details was a frequent task. Barrier and patrol road repairs and maintenance was an ongoing task. Mines and technical equipment had to be inspected, repaired and replaced. The control zone was periodically raked, and grass and brush was cut. This included work on the west side of the fence, accessed through gates or temporary gaps. Border markers and warning signs often had to be replaced as West German vandals would steal or deface them, which was against BRD law, but was not vigorously enforced. There were also local civilians from villages and collectives cultivating, caring for and harvesting crops and herding livestock. They were all watched by patrols. When large numbers of workers were present, especially when there were gaps in the fence or working on the fence's west side, guards would accompany the workers, be they *Grenztruppen* pioneers, contractors or farmers, and even established a line of guards between the workers and the border, sometimes just steps from the BRD border. BTR-152V armoured personnel carriers mounting machine guns might cover the workers.

Guard tower duty was another frequent assignment, but many were not continuously manned. The times they were occupied was varied. Those near towns, legal crossing stations and areas more easily accessible to escapees might be manned around the clock. In the late 1980s, when there were personnel shortages, cardboard silhouettes of guards were placed in towers to make them appear manned. Tower guards performed many of the same duties as foot patrols, maintaining surveillance over a specified area including to the flanks and rear, watching for activity in the West, and watching their own foot patrols. Besides normal binoculars, towers were sometimes provided more powerful mounted ones. Tower duty was obviously preferable to a foot patrol, avoiding rain or winter weather, although the towers were not heated. They could be hot in the summer and had no latrine.

Frontier crossing stations (GÜSt) on highways, railways and canals were manned by specially selected and trained personnel. They were trained to inspect all types of identity and transportation authorization documents. Those in the passport-control section were actually Stasi. They were conditioned to be extremely formal and serious, and permitted no exceptions to the strict regulations. There was actually a great deal of trade between East and West Germany via track, train and barge. Truck drivers travelled to both countries, their trucks marked 'TIR' (*Transports Internationaux Routiers*), a European customs agreement allowing trucks to cross borders with minimal customs formalities and no inspection. DDR trucks were operated by the state-owned VEB DEUTRANS and sometimes carried signal monitoring equipment and personnel. East German drivers frequently grew tired and

The two most common stances in which *Grenztruppen* were seen: either taking photographs or turning away from photographers. They are armed with MPiKM assault rifles. Note the green tabs on their rank shoulder straps, identifying them as *Grenztruppen* as opposed to NVA troops.

stopped for the night near NATO, Bundeswehr and government facilities. East German drivers knew that the authorities were alerted when they were to travel to the West, and it was made clear their families were virtually being held hostage until their return.

Western visitors were greeted by stoic guards who meticulously studied passport photographs and their resemblance to the bearers. Forms had to filled out declaring origin, destination, duration of visit, vehicle, quantities of cash carried, photographic equipment (restricted to East Germans) and much more. Vehicles were searched and a specified amount of Western money had to be exchanged for Ostmarks; this could not be re-exchanged when departing, to ensure that it was spent in the DDR.

Guards also manned control points entering the frontier zone to keep non-residents out and monitor the comings and goings of legal residents. They would check the identity cards of residents as they entered and departed. In some areas, when enough residents worked outside the frontier zone, special buses took them to and from work. Guards might ride along in either direction. During checks of passenger identification when the bus returned, drivers would alert the guard with a codeword if a suspected non-resident was on board.

Helicopter patrols were for general surveillance and a show of presence to the West. They seldom detected escapees, as they could be heard coming from afar. They were used to collect intelligence on activity in the West that could not be seen from ground level, followed suspicious vehicles, and delivered reaction forces. They were on occasion shot at by West German civilians, but with only small-calibre rifles or shotguns. Pilots had to take special care to remain on the east side of the border. The West Germans would make official complaints if violations occurred.

German Shepherd dogs (*deutscher Schaferhund*) were extensively used as watch, attack and tracking dogs. A frontier battalion typically had over a hundred dogs: 80–90 watch dogs, 6–8 attack dogs, two leashed tracking dogs, and a small pack of free-running tracking hounds. Each company and the battalion had an NCO service dog leader (*Deinsthundführer*) responsible for the dogs' care and training as well as the training of their handlers. The watch dogs were deployed on wire runs and in pens blocking fence gates. The tracking dogs were used to track individuals discovered in the frontier zone and the dog pack could be unleashed to pursue them. There were incidents in which innocent civilians and guards were mauled or killed by packs. The attack dogs were controlled by handlers and were often seen at crossing stations. The watch dogs were harshly treated and would even attack handlers. They were fed for one day during a 10-day period, sharpening their ferocity.

Each company possessed a specialized frontier reconnaissance platoon, the *Grenzaufklärungszug* (Gak). These were formed in the early 1970s and were initially of group (squad) strength, comprising 6–8 men. Gak platoons were often only 12–20 men. Their mission was to conduct low-level intelligence collection, daytime border surveillance, and maintained contact with informants among the frontier zone inhabitants. They worked closely with the Stasi branch. Gak members were recruited from the most politically reliable, physically fit, most professional career NCOs, and were required to be members of the Socialist Unity Party of Germany (*Sozialistische Einheitspartei Deutschlands,* SED). They underwent extensive Stasi background investigations and undertook eight hours of monthly special instruction by the regimental Stasi branch. The *Grenzaufklärengs* took a six-month course at the *Grenzaufklärungsschule* at Schiedungen in advanced reconnaissance, diversion techniques, espionage fieldcraft (ciphers, dead letter drops, agent contact means), photography, topography (maps, sketches, distance estimation), personal description techniques, first-aid, weapons, demolitions, hand-to-hand combat, survival training, and NATO unit organization, tactics and rank insignia. They were often the only company elements conducting daytime patrols while regular *Grenzer* patrolled at night. It was usually Gak personnel who operated in the zone west of the fence and guarded workers outside the fence while regular *Grenzer* watched from the inside. In the event of a NATO invasion, they were to detach themselves and operate as guerrillas, cooperating with Stasi agents and contacting West German sympathizers (most of whom were actually double agents intended to snare such activities). In 1983 the West German press claimed the DDR had dug four tunnels in unspecified locations to infiltrate reconnaissance personnel into the West to observe NATO troop movements and monitor radio traffic. This has never been validated.

A grave and memorial to those killed trying to cross from East to West Berlin, photographed in 1968. (IWM TR 30289-10)

Besides vigilance the guards relied on the electronic sensor fence, trip flares and dog-barking to alert them to escapes. If guards detected an apparent escapee or suspicious activity, they attempted to position themselves between the individual or activity and the border, prepared to make an arrest, and notified superiors. Pre-arranged 26mm coloured flares would be fired to signal whether a border penetration was being attempted from east to west or west to east.

The shooting order (*Shiessbehfel*) – Order 101 (*Befehl 101*) – had been in effect since at least 1948, but was not codified until 3 May 1974. However, all defecting *Grenzer* verified they were given full authority to fire on fleeing individuals for the following reasons:

• To prevent a crime or the continuation of a crime.
• When other methods to apprehend a frontier violator failed or were not possible.
• To protect against assaults or aggression.
• If an individual attempted to flee from an inspection or crossing station.
• If an arrested violator attempted to escape or disobey orders.
• When aircraft threatened frontier posts or landed in the DDR.

A 27 May 1952 *Grenzpolizei* order stated: 'Persons attempting to cross the control strip either in the direction of the DDR or of West Germany will be taken into custody. Failure to obey the orders of the Frontier Police will be met with the use of arms.'

If an individual was detected moving either west or east or was committing another crime the *Grenzer* ordered, 'Halt! Frontier sentry. Hands up!' (*'Halt! Grenzposten. Hände hoch!'*) or 'Halt, stand still, or I will shoot' (*'Halt, stehenbleiben, oder ich schieße!'*) If the individual did not comply with the order to halt, a warning shot was fired. If the individual still failed to comply, he was shot. If an escapee was between 100 and 300m away, where he would be unable to hear the order to halt, he could be shot without warning. There were instances when individuals were discovered about to escape into the West, that is, already on the west side of the fence, and were shot without warning. Guards attempting to flee could be shot without verbal warning or a warning shot. Guards were not to fire if innocent bystanders on either side of the border might be hit, particularly women and children, or when the situation no longer allowed it – that is, the escapee had made it to BRD territory. They were not to fire if the line of fire was into the BRD, although this often occurred. Fortunately, the only weapons employed were submachine guns and assault rifles, usually on semi-automatic mode, rather than heavy-calibre machine guns.

A detained individual would be informed: 'You are under arrest. If you try and escape we will use our weapons.' He would be searched, restrained and taken to the company headquarters where he would be turned over to the Stasi. Escapees were known to have killed guards. Arrested escapees faced up to three years in prison, later increased to eight, plus fines. Other charges were often added, such as smuggling and assault, and sentences could be much longer, but could be as little as two years. Once released from prison they would have difficulty finding employment. *Grenzer* attempting to defect received six years for desertion.

Most guards looked forward to the end of their 18-months' service. Westerners would watch passing guards proudly hold up a knotted string stretched between their hands to show how much time they had remaining. A new knot was tied each day for the last 30 days of service.

TESTING THE BARRIERS

There is little doubt that the Wall and the IGB were effective in halting the flight to the West. The IGB was porous into the 1960s, but with each passing year it became more formidable. By the mid-1970s it had become extremely risky to attempt escape. The flow gradually slowed, but nonetheless the bold, resourceful, and crafty would continue to try and sometimes succeeded.

They jumped from windows, crawled through sewers, swam rivers and lakes, hid in concealed vehicle compartments, cut through fences, and made desperate dashes across deadly ground and through mines to clamber over barriers under spotlights and gunfire. Thousands made it out and hundreds died trying. Others crashed trucks, tractors and automobiles through fences and gates. One man even built a mini-tank to break through. Another built a mini-submarine and escaped through the Baltic in 1986. In 1979 two families made it out in a hot air balloon. This resulted in the restriction of vinyl sheeting sales in the East. In 1962 a group of students dug a tunnel from West to East Berlin and brought out 28 people before it flooded. A few tunnels were dug from east to west. In 1986 a man modified and painted a car to look like a Soviet vehicle, made three mannequins with Soviet uniforms, and bluffed his way through a checkpoint.

Escapees were shot down in cold blood in full view of West Berliners. There were incidents in which the *Grenztruppen* allowed wounded escapees to bleed to death lying where they fell. In one incident, two West Berlin children fell in the River Spree and drowned; the *Grenztruppen* provided no assistance and did not allow West Berliners to enter the river. Westerners began to exploit the situation, charging East Germans up to 40,000 marks to smuggle them out in hidden vehicle compartments, with false papers, or through tunnels.

An estimated 3,700,000 left East Germany between the end of World War II and 1961. From August 1961 to the end of 1962, 14,268 people escaped. In 1964, 3,155 escaped with 2,699 following in 1972. Improved barriers allowed only 969 to make it out in 1976. In 1985, 160 escaped. In all some 2,500 NVA personnel escaped, of which 90 per cent were *Grenzer*.

The fall of the Wall

The events leading up the fall of the Wall – *die Wende* (the turning point) – are complex. The economic situation in the DDR and other Warsaw Pact states was quickly deteriorating in the 1980s. Secretary Mikhail Gorbachev of the USSR had enacted the *perestroika* policy, the restructuring of the economy, in 1985. At the same time he introduced *glasnost*, the beginning of a new 'openness' within the Soviet government. The plans failed in the goal of making the USSR economically competitive on a worldwide basis, resulting in *catastroika* and the downfall of Communism. He had weakened the system of internal political repression. The Warsaw Pact states were also seeking economic reform and increased personal liberties. The DDR president, Erich Honecker, remained resolute, declaring in January 1989: 'The Wall will be there in 50 years, even 100 years.' The new openness in the East led Hungary to declare the 1956 uprising was justified and it opened its borders. Thousands of East Germans poured into Hungary on tourist visas and then to Austria from September 1989. Poland too opened its borders. Anti-regime protests spread, with many East Germans declaring they would stay and demanding a new government. Gorbachev met with the DDR leadership between 7 and 9 October for the 40th anniversary of the state's establishment, and made clear that the USSR would not interfere in the DDR's affairs. He stated, 'Those who delay are punished by life itself.'

The German flag flying over the reopened Brandenburg Gate, above a graffiti-covered Berlin Wall. The Gate was opened on 22 December 1989. (IWM CT 1492)

The leaders were on their own, and to delay the inevitable would only make matters worse. On 17 October the DDR *Politbüro* replaced Honecker, who proposed repressing the protests, with Egon Krenz. Krenz would be ousted in December and replaced by Hans Modrow, who promised the people reforms but with the retention of a socialist government.

Protests continued, and it was realized that the situation was out of control. A *Politbüro* member, Guenther Schabowski, mistakenly announced the opening of the checkpoints on 9 November. He went on to say that the regulation took effect immediately. No instructions had been given to the *Grenztruppen* and a dangerous situation developed as thousands of Berliners on both sides congregated. In a festive atmosphere people began climbing the Wall. The confused guards stood to the side, often pelted with stones and bottles. Gates were torn down, ladders went up, and sledgehammers and then jackhammers were turned on the hated Wall. Along the IGB, events were much the same. Thousands of East Germans flooded into towns on the west side, and were welcomed as guests. Families were reunited. Germany changed overnight and the Iron Curtain crashed down. The Wall remained physically, but its time as a barrier was over. On 22 December the Brandenburg Gate was opened, the symbolic gateway to the East. The next day visa-free travel for West and East Germans was authorized.

On 18 March the Unification Treaty was signed by the BRD and DDR. There were still symbolic border controls in a futile effort by the DDR to control trade, but amid protest the controls were lifted on 30 June. The next day the *Grenztruppen* was dissolved. At the end of August the Treaty on the Establishment of a Unified Germany was agreed, followed by the Unification Treaty Act on 23 September. On 3 October Germany and Berlin were reunited (*deutsche Wiedervereinigung*).

AN ASSESSMENT OF THE WALL AND THE IGB

The building of the Wall and the fortified border separating the two Germanys proved to be a political, social and economic disaster for the DDR, the Warsaw Pact, and the USSR. The Wall became a symbol of Communist tyranny. However, for the most part the Wall and the IGB fulfilled their rolls. They reduced the escapes of professionals, educated and skilled workers to a trickle, stabilized and controlled population movement, reduced illegal money exchange, allowed the unhindered 'development' of the socialist economy, reduced the fear of Western agent penetrations, and fended off the encroachment of Western ideals of democracy and capitalism. The cost was massive for a country strapped for money and resources. Much of the material used in the frontier barriers had to be purchased from other countries – even from the West. The maintenance of almost 50,000 *Grenztruppen* plus the additional manning of the various police and security organs kept thousands of able-bodied men out of the already limited labour pool.

While costly, the barriers and security systems backing them were relatively effective, but were far from efficient, owing to the extensive need for manpower, limited numbers of remote sensors and surveillance systems, often poor materials, and the demand for constant maintenance. The Wall and the IGB do not represent an effective model for any modern barrier

DDR escapee casualties

Location	Prior to 13 August 1961	From 13 August 1961	Total
Berlin Wall	16	239	**255**
Intra-German Border	100	271	**371**
Baltic Sea	15	174	**189**
Other borders	3	41	**44**
En route (on airplanes, autobahn)	–	7	**7**
Grenzpolizist, Grenztruppen	11	16	**27**
Soviet Army deserters	1	5	**6**
Aircraft engagement in frontier area	14	3	**17**
Total	**160**	**756**	**916**

The footprints of escapees across the control strip. The foot-patrol path can be seen along the left edge of the control strip.

The 27 November 1961 Checkpoint Charlie stand off, when four US M48A1 Patton tanks (three with dozer blades) faced ten Soviet T-54 tanks, brought the world to the threshold of another war. The small checkpoint hut can be seen in the centre of Friedrichstraße.

system, as technology has moved on in the last 30 years. However, similarities with the IGB can be identified in the Israeli West Bank and Gaza Strip walls, the largely ineffective barriers on the US–Mexican border, the Moroccan Western Sahara Wall, the modest Thai–Malay barrier, and others.

After the fall, *Grenztruppen*, Stasi and Vopo records were examined to determine who had shot escapees. While the actions of Stasi undercover agents were declared exempt from criminal prosecution by BRD courts, murder or manslaughter charges were brought against surviving guards and police, who were declared 'death shooters' (*Todesschützen*). Most sentences were suspended.

Lists of those who died on the Wall and the IGB are seldom in agreement. A running list was maintained, but when the DDR files were opened it was found that many records had been destroyed, and significant numbers of previously unknown casualties were discovered. The figures on page 59 are debatable, as other sources list significantly different numbers. One claims 85 *Grenzpolizist/Grenztruppen* were killed attempting to escape.

A total of 29 *Grenzpolizist* and *Grenztruppen* were killed on duty. Of these, eight died on the Berlin Wall and one on the Czechoslovak border. The circumstances of their deaths are not always known. While some were indeed killed by escapees and possibly suicide, most are believed to have been shot accidentally by guards, accidentally killed by mines, or shot attempting to escape. The actual circumstances of the latter deaths were not reported. Those who died under 'honourable' circumstances were heralded as 'frontier protectors' (*Grenzschützer*) and exploited for propaganda purposes, with schools, barracks, roads, holiday and cultural houses, and pioneer camps named after them.

The monetary cost of the barriers was high. To improve the still-crude IGB in 1961–64 cost 1,822 million Ostmarks, while another 400 million were expended on the Berlin Wall. It is estimated that some 500 million a year were spent to improve and maintain the Wall and the IGB plus another 38 million Ostmarks for Stasi passport-control operations.

Barriers and facilities removed by January 1994 (in km)			
Barriers/facilities	**IGB**	**Berlin Wall**	**Total**
Walls	31.83	178.63	210.46
Fences (all types)	2,564.48	297.07	2,861.55
Barbed-wire obstacles	86.25	8	94.25
Anti-vehicle ditches (concrete-reinforced)	638.5	84.99	723.49
Anti-vehicle ditches (un-reinforced)	51.78	–	51.78
Patrol roads	559.66	119.39	697.05
Lighting systems	237.31	160.13	397.44
Floodlight lines	91.6	–	91.6
Dog runs	170.2	6.6	176.8
Towers	538	255	793
Bunkers	48	–	48
Bridges (patrol road)	89	12	101
Water obstacles	168	7	175

Notes Source: *Engineer Magazine*, August 1994. All numbers provided are in kilometres.
Note that some small portions of barriers and three towers were retained for historical purposes.

THE SITES TODAY

The Berlin Wall was mostly removed within a year of its fall, although the 'country wall' remained for a longer period. Many Berlin residents on either side of the disappeared Wall now have difficulty recalling its trace. New buildings and streets were built in the old cleared security zone while old adjacent buildings were demolished and replaced. In some areas a double line of bricks are set in concrete following the Wall's trace. A complete 212m section of the control zone was rebuilt near Checkpoint Charlie – the Bemauer Straße Memorial – with all the walls, fences, patrol road, anti-vehicle ditch etc., but this is not on the original site. Graffiti-daubed Grenzwall 75 elements can still be found around the city (and indeed around the world), either left in place or relocated. The 1,316m-long East Side Gallery is a segment of Grenzwall 75 featuring 106 paintings. Only three towers remain. There are five Berlin Wall museums and display sites in Berlin. Souvenir pieces of the Wall can often be found on sale – although their authenticity can be doubtful.

Similarly, the IGB has all but disappeared. The German Army contracted firms (staffed by unemployed *Grenzers* and NVA soldiers) to dismantle the barriers, clear mined areas, reconnect roads and autobahns, and return the restricted zone to its natural state. There are at least 30 public, private and local municipality museums and IGB-related sites along the trace of the border. Displays of mesh fences, signal fences, patrol roads, towers and bunkers can all be found. The Frontier Land Museum (Grenzland-Museum) at Eichsfeld provides examples of most barriers and facilities. In Mödlareuth ('Little Berlin') parts of the wall dividing the town remain.

In 1989 the development of the Green Belt of Germany (*Grünes Band Deutschland*) commenced. However, environmental protesters noted that the strip of land following the IGB trace had remained untouched since 1952, and campaigned to have a 100m strip of the trace, or at least specific areas, designated nature preserves with a hike and bike trail running its length. The European Parliament has called for a similar trail running the entire length of the Iron Curtain.

There are still some cultural differences between *Wessis* and *Ossis*. Many East Germans have found the transition to free-market capitalism and the democratic process a difficult process. What is known as *die Mauer im Kopf* (the Wall in the head) remains. A 2004 poll found that 25 per cent of West Germans and 12 per cent of East Germans wished the Wall was still there. Even today, some *Ossis* demonstrate a nostalgia for the *ancien régime*, cherishing mementos, real and reproduced, of their former lives.

FURTHER READING AND RESEARCH

Bailey, Anthony, *Along the Edge of the Forest: An Iron Curtain Journey* (NY: Random House, 1983)

Baumgarten, Klaus-Dieter and Freitag, Peter, *Die Grenzen Der DDR* (Berlin: Edition Ost, 2004)

Buckley, William F., Jr, *The Fall of the Berlin Wall* (Hoboken, NY: John Wiley and Sons, 2004)

Forester, Thomas M., *The East German Army: Second in the Warsaw Pact* (London: George Allen & Unwin, 1980)

Funder, Anna, *Stasiland: True Stories from Behind the Berlin Wall* (London: Granta Books, 2003)

The fate of many parts of the Berlin Wall – this section was acquired by the Imperial War Museum, London, UK, and is now on display in its grounds in Lambeth. (Nikolai Bogdanovic)

Lapp, Peter J., *Die Grenztruppen der DDR: Frontdienst im Frieden* (Koblenz: Bernard u. Graefe, 1986)

Stacy, William C., *US Army Border Operations in Germany, 1945–1983* (HQ, US Army Europe and Seventh Army, Military History Office, 1984)

Taylor, Frederick, *The Berlin Wall: A World Divided, 1961–1989* (New York: Harper Collins, 2007)

Thoss, Hendrik, *Gesichert in den Untergang: Die Geschichte der DDR-Westgrenze* (Berlin: Dietz Verlag, 2004)

WEBSITES
www.die-berliner-mauer.de/en/index.html – 'Retracing the Wall'.
http://grenze.com – examines the *Grenztruppen*.
www.websauger.eu – The Berlin Wall and the IGB.
www.nachkriegsmuseen.de/grenze.html – Museums of the Wall and IGB.

GLOSSARY AND ABBREVIATIONS

German	English	German	English
Bayerische Grenzpolizei	Bavarian Frontier Police	*Kontrollzone*	Control Zone
Berliner Mauer	Berlin Wall (*die Mauer*)	*Landgrenze*	Land Frontier (IGB)
Bundesgrenzschutz	Federal Frontier Protection	*Ministerium des Innern* (MdI)	Ministry of the Interior
Bundesrepublik Deutschland (BRD)	Federal Republic of Germany – West Germany	*Ministerium für Staatssicherheit* (MfS)	Ministry for State Security – the Stasi
Bundeszollverwaltung	Federal Customs Administration	*Nationale Volksarmee* (NVA)	National People's Army
Deutsche Demokratische Republik (DDR)	German Democratic Republic – East Germany	NATO	North Atlantic Treaty Organization
Deutsche Grenzpolizei (DGP)	German Frontier Police	*Republikflucht*	Republic desertion (escapes)
die Grenz	the Frontier	*Schießbefehl*	Shooting Order
Grenzer	Frontier guard	*Schultzzone*	Security Zone
Grenzgesetz	Frontier Statute	*Sperrzone*	Restricted Zone
Grenztruppen der DDR	Frontier Troops of the DDR	*Übergangs*	crossing points
Grenzübergangsstelle (GÜSt)	Frontier Crossing Station	*Volkspolizei* (Vopo)	People's Police
IGB	Intra-German Border	*Zonengrenze*	Frontier Zone
Innerdeutsche Grenze	Intra-German Frontier (a.k.a. *Deutsch-Deutsche Grenze*)	*Zonenrandförderung*	Zonal Border Order

Using a hammer and chisel, a child removes a fragment of the Berlin Wall after the opening of the passages on 9 November 1989. By the end of 1990, much of the Wall had been demolished. (IWM CT 1493)

INDEX

References to illustrations are shown in bold. Plates are shown with page and caption locators in brackets.